We Preach

Stephen R. Melton

Parson's Porch Books

We Preach

ISBN: Softcover 978-1-951472-16-0

Copyright © 2016 by Stephen R. Melton

All rights reserved. No part of this book may be reproduced or transmitted in any form or by any means, electronic or mechanical, including photocopying, recording, or by any information storage and retrieval system, without permission in writing from the publisher.

Cover Art Credit: From *La Passion de Nostre Seigneur* by Jehan Gerson (Pierre de Tatras: 1960)

To order additional copies of this book, contact:

Parson's Porch Books
1-423-475-7308
www.parsonsporch.com

Parson's Porch Books is an imprint of Parson's Porch & Company (PP&C) in Cleveland, Tennessee. PP&C is an innovative company which raises money by publishing books of noted authors, representing all genres. All donations from contributors and profits from publishing are shared with the poor.

We Preach

Table of Contents

Dedication 9

Epigraph

A Poem, "We Preach" 11

Advent

The Axe Is At The Roots 13
  Matthew 3: 1-12
Preparation 18
  Matthew 25: 1-13
Defining Christmas 23
  Titus 3: 1-11
Speaking Without Words 27
  John 1: 1-18

Christmas

Saying, "Yes" to God 30
  Luke 1: 38

Epiphany

Going Home By Another Way 34
  Matthew 2: 1-18

Valentine's Day

Two Loves, One God 38
  Song of Solomon 2: 10-14; John 15: 9-13

Lent

The Last Temptation of Christ   42
Matthew 4: 1-11

Maundy Thursday

I love you. Eat.   48
John 16: 16-24; John 17: 20- 26

Palm Sunday

Palm Sunday Lament   52
Matthew 21: 1-11

Easter

Running to the Tomb   55
John 20: 1-18

Pentecost

How Will We Speak?   59
Genesis 11: 1-9; Acts 2: 1-8

Christ Our King Sunday

Taraxacum asteracea   63
John 12: 9-19

Mother's Day

Whispered Love   67
       I John 4: 7-21

Graduate Recognition

Success   71
       Matthew 19: 23-30; Proverbs 11: 24-28

Labor Day

The Blessing of Work   75
       II Thessalonians 3: 6-18

Stewardship Sunday

What Size Potatoes Are We Planting?   79
       Luke 17: 11-19

Baptism

Remember the Image   83
       Mark 1: 9-11

Ordinary Days

Taking A Risk   87
       Matthew 25: 14-30

Attractive Prayer Mark 4: 35-41;	91
Something Happened Exodus 14: 5-31	95
How Beautiful Are the Feet... Romans 10: 11-15	99
About the Author	103

Dedication

I heard a story about two guys talking about sermons. The first guy is complaining about preachers and their sermons: "I went to church for years but I forgot the sermon by the next day. So, I figured, 'What's the use in going to church and listening to a sermon if I can't even remember it a day later?'" The other fellow says, "You know I can't recall anything I had to eat this week but something tells me I did eat. In fact, if I hadn't eaten, I would have noticed that. I can't help but think sermons are like that. Even if I don't remember them for long, it doesn't mean they didn't do me some good. They feed me despite the fact I can't recall all the words."

This book is dedicated to pastors who labor each Sunday to find a way to nourish their congregations. No doubt some meals (i.e. sermons) are better than others, but thanks be to God for preachers who want to provide a meal each week for the parishioners looking for something to sustain them for the week, or perhaps, just for an hour.

EPIGRAPH

We Preach

Seeds float in the air.
They find their home in fertile soil.
They grow and mature; they take on a life of their own leaving behind the seed, but the seed is still there.
We preach from seeds that float in the air,
riding on the breath of God.
Sometimes preaching is picking up the seeds that land on our doorstep.
We get them like we get the wind and the rain;
they come to the just and the unjust.
Sometimes preaching is a relentless dig through the packets of seeds at the garden store.
There are so many.
Which one do we choose?
Sometimes the seed falls on fertile soil.
We plant it and it grows and it becomes a sermon which nourishes the faithful.
Praise be to God!
Sometimes the seed falls on barren ground.
There it is.
We see it.
But we can do nothing with it.
It can do nothing with us.
It has been a hard week.
The Session grilled us.
The family is mad at us.
The Adversary is asking us again,
"And why are you doing this for a living?"
Sometimes the seed looks better than it is.
We plant it and nothing happens.
We stare at it through the print on the screen and it stares back --
nothing.
We try again.
What makes for the fertile ground of faith?

Maybe it is praying.
Maybe it is reading the Bible.
Maybe it is love.
Maybe what makes for the fertile soil of faith is ground so dry, in such desperate need of rain, that we have to say,
"Lord, we have nothing; we are nothing. We are empty."
We are silent.
God is silent.
And we wait.
And then the rain falls.
In a gentle mist or in a spring torrent.
The water comes.
The ground drinks in thirsty gulps and the seed grows.
And one more Sunday,
we preach.

- Stephen R. Melton

ADVENT

The Axe Is at The Roots
Matthew 3: 1-12

John the Baptist isn't the most adorable person, is he? I was looking at a picture which came with a children's bulletin. John the Baptist is a cartoon character with a big smile. I think how different this must be from the real John the Baptist?! We tend to favor other characters in the Bible: Noah and the ark, Daniel in the lion's den, Paul preaching to beat the band, even lesser known people like Abigail and Ruth; they stir us. John the Baptist just scares us! If not for his street-corner type preaching, then for his diet of bugs and honey. We don't get the sense John ever abided by the notion, "Cleanliness is next to godliness." But the fact that all four of the Gospel mention him means we probably should give him his day.

I suppose one of the things which bothers us about John the Baptist, is he seems rather narrow-minded and his message doesn't vary much at all. John has one message: "Repent!" - that's it. No other choices. Change! Repent! John was not only singular, he was imperative. Especially at this time of year…Jesus and Santa Claus seem to have something in common but John is like the Grinch who stole Christmas. Jesus was opening doors, and surprising people with choices. John says there is no other choice. <u>Either stop what we are doing now – right now – or it may be too late</u>. The axe is at the root and soon the tree will fall. Make a choice!

What's so difficult is we live in a time which worships choice. We don't believe people should be forced to choose this or that. We believe in options. If you don't believe that, count all the different kinds of cereals next time you go shopping.

We like choices.

Not just for our cereals and our laundry soap, we like choices for even the most important things in life, like our faith and what we believe. This is why John the Baptist doesn't make sense to most of us. When John says, "Repent!" – he is implying that the choices we are making now may, well, be wrong.

While we may believe that with all the choices we have, and all the options to choose – I mean, although it is nice to have fifty different kinds of cereal and laundry soap – do we really believe one choice is better than another? Not really – it's all a matter of taste. So, maybe we start to believe that about *all* the choices we make? You see?

If one decision is no better than another, than maybe even what we believe about faith and morality and how to treat one another, doesn't really matter. Well, John says it does matter and there are some choices we need to turn away from so we can turn towards the ones which matter.

See the word, *"decision,"* comes from the Latin word meaning, *"to cut off or to sever."* So, it's often true, when we make a decision, when we decide to do this or that, we do cut ourselves off from all the other decisions we could have made. When we decide, it is like going through a door which locks behind us. We are not sure we want to do that. We don't especially want to narrow our options. We'd rather keep that door ajar.

Why go on record saying we love someone when there is a chance we may love someone else or someone else might love us better? Why go on record standing up for something we think is right, when we might discover we are wrong? Why choose to join a church when there are so many churches out there? The same with religion itself - why say we are Christian when maybe the Buddhist's have it right?

Why make a decision for anything because we might discover that something else may be better - especially knowing that when we do make a decision we cut ourselves off from all the other decisions we might have made?

Like the story of the Presbyterian minister who died and went to heaven. St. Peter met him at the Gate and said, "Your first choice is to choose one of these two doors. The first door is heaven. The second door is a discussion about heaven." The minister, not wanting to commit himself too quickly, choose the *discussion*.

There is an old saying which may apply here: "If we stand up for nothing, we will fall for anything." You see, though it may be true that making a decision means we have cut ourselves off from other options, it also means when we do make a choice, we have just opened a door to all the goodness only that decision can provide. People who live together may have blessings, but there are even deeper blessings for people who are able to make a life-time commitment.

When John said, "Repent!" he was saying, "Make a choice!" Make a choice today, because, after all, we may not have all the time in the world to make another choice.

Making choices involves risk for sure, but living as if we can put off making commitments may have even greater peril.

A few years ago a church member of mine asked me to attend the funeral of her step-father. He was not a kind man. In fact, he had abused her as a child. But, she felt out of respect for her mother, she would go to the funeral. She asked if I would go with her for moral support, so I did.

The funeral was at a little Independent Baptist Church somewhere is the backwoods of Kentucky. It was a hot day and the church was crowded. They wheeled the coffin in and then the preacher began to preach. At first, it was no different than a 100 other funerals I had been too, then, it changed.

The preacher was only into his sermon a few words when he took a totally different tone. He started to shout: "We all know it's too late for Sam! He may have wanted to make his life better, but it's too late for him now, he's dead! He's gone now."

I remember being stunned. I was thinking to myself, "Wow, not much comfort to his grieving family - what in heaven's name could be worse than this?" - and then it got worse.

The preacher stepped down from the pulpit and started talking to the people in the pews. He knew them by name. He looked at one man and said, "And you, Earl, you know what I am saying. You know you need to get your life right, because it may be too late for you too soon!" Then, he turned his attention to another man farther back in the pews, "And you Charlie, it's time, and you know it. You have wasted too much on drinking and not being home!"

Then, I got really nervous, because he started walking towards me. Naturally, as a Presbyterian, I was sitting in the back pew. He came closer and closer, and honest to God, I started to sweat, "Dear God," I thought, "What is he going to say to me?" Maybe it was the heat or maybe I had a guilty conscience, or maybe it was the Holy Spirit but I felt like God was right there in the room.

He looked at me and then he looked at the others and said, "Sam might have wanted to straighten out his life, but he didn't and he can't now. It's over. It's too late for him…But, it's not too late for you. People drop dead every day. Now is the time to make your life count for something. Stop being foolish! Turn to Jesus!"

Then, he said a prayer and we sang a song and it was over.

When I got home, I told a minister friend of mine about what happened. I said, "I think that was the worst thing I ever saw. Can you imagine a preacher doing something like that? It was so manipulative. I would never preach a sermon like that.

My friend agreed that it was tacky, manipulative and callous, but, he said, "Of course, the worst part is it happens to be true."

John the Baptist couldn't have said it better: "The axe is at the roots. Every tree that does not bear fruit will be cut down and thrown into the fire!" It may not be the happiest Merry Christmas message in the world, but, then again, it isn't Christmas yet, it's Advent. And, of course, as much as we might not like John's blunt message, it just so happens to be true. We don't know when our final hour will come. John was right. The axe is at the roots. It may not sell a lot of Christmas cards, but it is truth nonetheless.

TO GOD BE THE GLORY FOREVER AND EVER. AMEN.

Preparation
Matthew 25: 1-13

Be prepared. Seems like we spend most of our lives preparing for something, don't we? Getting ready for school, getting ready for work, if we are lucky, we are getting ready for a vacation. These days we are preparing for Christmas.

I was reading a book on mountain climbing and I came upon an interesting quote. The author said there are many times life throws unexpected things our way and we just have to do our best, In fact, there are lots of things in this life which happen by accident but climbing a mountain isn't one of them. We don't climb a mountain by accident. It is one of those things we have to make an intentional decision to do.

I don't know if it's true, but often some of the most important things in life take preparation. Maybe that gives us something to think about when it comes to our faith?

Of course, preparation – no matter what kind we are talking about - is one of those things WE have to do. Preparation doesn't happen automatically. No one is really born ready. We have to decide to become ready.

We didn't realize it until after she died, but my mother was one for being prepared. We discovered this as we were going through her things. As we were picking up we found her purse. Opening it was like opening a time capsule – a freeze frame of her life the moment she died. Inside the purse we found these things: Vit. E cream, compact Aqua Net hair spray, a collapsible cup, lock de-icer (and this was in September), sugar, lemon juice, address book, calendar, memo pads, dictionary, brush, K-mart name tag, chapstick, suckers, clippers, scissors, 4" rule, toothbrush, paint can opener, breath freshener, a pocket cross and other assorted items.

This is a true story.

Safe to say my mother believed in being prepared. You just might need lock de-icer in September, or someone might walk up to you and say, "Hey, I was going to paint my house, do you have a paint can opener on ya?" My mother could proudly say for all the unprepared to hear, "Why, yes, I have that right here." Suckers were for unexpected grandkids who stopped by. Who knows what the dictionary was for? I guess you never know when we might have to spell something?

Be prepared. Perhaps one lesson she learned in life was that you'd better be prepared because, other than God, we only have ourselves to depend upon for certain things and, if we are not prepared, we are stuck. So, she made herself ready.

Preparedness is something we choose.

Of course, the parable today about the ten maidens is about preparation. Five maidens were wise and brought oil and five maidens were foolish and didn't bring enough.

Oil is a metaphor for preparation in the Bible. Oil was used to prepared alters for worship. Moses used oil to prepare sacrifices. The women came bringing oil to prepare Jesus' body for burial.

Jesus tells the parable as a way of saying that we need to be prepared. He is saying we need to be prepared so we can see the good stuff of life.

Now, that all makes some sense to us, even if we weren't a Boy Scout. We know the wisdom in being prepared, so there is nothing new here, but there is something bothersome about the parable when the five foolish maidens ask for help.

Think about it?

The ten maidens are getting ready for the feast. The first five brought enough oil to burn all night, but the other five didn't. The groom happens to be a little late, as grooms have been known to do. When the five foolish maidens realize they are running out of oil, naturally, they ask the five wise maidens to share theirs.

BUT here is where the five **wise** maidens sound more like the five **selfish** maidens. "No way," they say. "If we share with you, there won't be enough for us. Go buy some of your own." So, the foolish maidens rush out to The Dollar General to get some oil. They run back to the party, but when they do, the door is locked and no one will let them in. The groom yells, "I don't know you. Go away." The door is shut and they are excluded, unrecognized, unwanted.

And what is bothersome is when Jesus says, "Thus is the kingdom of God." Something about this sounds terrible, doesn't it? Didn't we learn somewhere that the kingdom of God is about sharing, about helping people when they need help? Isn't God's grace unconditional and isn't the door ALWAYS opened to those who knock?

Remember that other parable when Jesus told of the woman who kept knocking on the door of the judge until he finally let her in? (Luke 11:10) Jesus affirmed her persistence. And, Jesus said, "Seek and ye shall find. Knock and the door will be opened." But, obviously not this time. In this parable, the ones who seek are turned away and the ones who knock are ignored. The ones who are rewarded, are those huddled inside, who wouldn't share their oil. They are the ones who get to go to the party. It's a little disturbing. It seems to praise self-interest, maybe even selfishness.

But, you see, the five wise maidens were right, weren't they? There are some things we can share in this life, but we cannot share the oil of preparation. We are the only ones responsible for our own lives. We are the ones who need to prepare ourselves for life, whether in financial matters, emotional challenges or spiritual growth. WE are the ones have to oversee our own lives. It is true that other people can help us from time to time, but it is not up to other people to take care of us. We are responsible for our own preparation.

See, the foolish maidens assumed that someone would take care of them. They believed someone would make sure they were ready. "If we run out of oil, our friends will help. If we are gone when the groom arrives, he will wait. If he does go in, he will surely let us in."

We are responsible for our own spiritual welfare. Jesus was talking about all of life, no doubt, but, you better know he was talking about our soul. He was telling us - We make the choices of whether we *grow in faith* or *wither in indifference.*

So, we ask ourselves: "Are we doing the things we need to do to prepare ourselves for God?"

Let me tell you another story about mother before she learned to be prepared. When I was younger and my father was alive, our whole family attended a church in Southern Indiana. After my father died and we moved away, some ten years later, my mother still hadn't moved her church membership. I think she held onto her membership because it reminded her of better times when my father was alive – it was a connection to the past. As time passed, more and more of those connections to my father faded and broke loose and that was hard. Well, one day she got a letter from her former church telling her she had been removed from the church rolls. They had not seen in her worship and she had not supported the church financially, so they figured she had simply moved on.

I remember how she was angry that they took her off the rolls. I mean she fussed and fussed about how that church was only interested in money and so on. But, I couldn't help but wonder if her church was so important to her, why hadn't she at least sent in a few dollars to let them know how important her church was to her? Wasn't the Christian thing to do - to just leave her on the rolls? Not really. Because in leaving her on the rolls it sent the message that she could be apathetic about her religious life and that was ok. At a deeper level, it kept her clinging to the past.

The good news was that after being upset for a bit, she decided that maybe it was time for her to become involved in a church where we lived. Up until then, she hadn't made a commitment to any church. But that letter, as disturbing as it was for her, was one of the best things that could happen. It made her realize it was time for her to take responsibility for her spiritual life and get involved in a church again.

We are the ones responsible for nurturing our souls. Other people can help us, but ultimately, it is our calling. Our souls are like a engine that need oil. Without the oil, the engine freezes up. Without nurturing our souls our souls freeze up. I think Jesus is telling us we are the ones responsible for our walk with God. No one can do that for us. Now is the time to prepare our souls. Let us light our lamp and ready ourselves that God may come in.

TO GOD BE THE GLORY FOREVER AND EVER. AMEN.

Defining Christmas
Titus 3: 1-11

In 1925, the New York World magazine celebrated the birthday of Abraham Lincoln with a cartoon. It showed two Kentucky farmers talking over a picket fence. One says, "Anything happen lately?" The other responds, "Nothing much. Just a new baby born over at Tom Lincoln's place."

I am sure there were folks who said the same thing in Bethlehem that first Christmas night. Standing on the corner just outside the inn, one says, "Anything happen lately?" "Naw, just some baby born back in the stable. Although there did seem to be more shepherds back there than animals."

Things are a little different nowadays. Christmas may have come in secret the first time, but now we see it coming for months away. Remember when we never saw anything about Christmas until after Thanksgiving? Now decorations start popping up in Walmart at Halloween. No hiding Christmas anymore.

But, you know, the problem is that although we may see Christmas coming, we may not know what it means when it gets here? I remember watching the *Today Show*. Matt Lauhr was interviewing a teacher who had agreed to give a kidney to a young boy in her class who desperately needed one to live. As he was thanking her for the interview, he said something that caught my attention, "You know we often find it hard to <u>define</u> the spirit of Christmas, but it seems to me what you are doing exemplifies it."

At first I thought that was odd, "We find it hard to <u>define</u> the spirit of Christmas..." "Define"? I thought to myself, "Christmas is about the birth of Jesus, of course. What's so hard to define?" But, maybe we understand his question. Don't we sometimes feel Christmas has been hijacked and it's hard to hold onto the meaning? The humorist, Garrison Keillor, of the "Prairie Home Companion," talks about the time one of his characters, Pastor Ingquist, went to the mall to buy gifts for his kids. As he walked into the warehouse-sized store, he finds himself wondering, "Why, for heavens sakes, am I buying a video game called, *Annihilation*, for Christmas?" So, we can see Christmas coming, but the meaning flies right by us with the speed of a miniature sleigh and eight tiny reindeer.

When thinking about the best way to define Christmas, I decided to research how Christmas began. You see, Christmas was not considered sacred until about 300 years after Jesus' birth. The word Christmas means, "Christ's Mass" - the name for the worship service the evening before Christmas. The first Christ's Mass took place around 1036.

We don't really know why December 25 was chosen as the date of Christ's birth. It seems unlikely that Christ was born in winter because shepherds would not be herding their flocks out in the cold, and, although Caesar's are notoriously inconsiderate, it is unlikely they would arrange for a world-wide census during one of the darkest and chilliest months of the year. Most experts guess that Jesus was probably born in April or May.

The best guess for why December 25 was chosen for the date of Christ's birth was because it was close to the winter Solstice - the day the sun begins to shine longer and the days of light lengthen. Pagan religions would celebrate the return of the sun, spelled, **S-U-N**. The Christian church wanted to steal attention away from the pagan holiday so they declared this just so happens to be the day the Son, spelled, **S-O-N**, came to earth.

Christmas was not always a popular holiday, especially in America. Believe it or not, there was a period of time from 1659 to 1681 when Christmas was outlawed by the Puritans in Boston. The Puritans were so opposed to Christmas because they knew about its pagan roots. So, for centuries Christmas was pretty much overlooked. It wasn't until after the Civil War people began to send cards. The turning point was December 24, 1867 when Macy's department store in New York remained open until midnight. After that, commercialism took hold of Christmas.

The practice of giving gifts goes back to the **Wise Men** who brought gold, frankincense and myrrh for the baby Jesus. We celebrate twelve days of Christmas because it was supposedly on January 6 - 12 days after Christ was born - that the Wise Men finally found Jesus. To use a star to find a particular house is not the most exact method. It may be just another way of saying they were traveling by faith.

I remember receiving a card which said: "If the Three Wise Men had been women, 1) They wouldn't have been late. 2) If they had gotten lost, they would have stopped and asked directions. 3) They would have brought something more practical like diapers or a casserole."

That's some of the information I got from my research about Christmas.

It may not tell us a lot on the surface, but there is something about what the Wise men did which does seem different from what we do today.

Here is the difference. While the Wise Men brought gifts to give to others – perfect strangers – Christmas has become a reason for us to buy stuff for ourselves. And, by "ourselves," I mean our circle of friends and our family.

Maybe the real meaning of Christmas is in what the Wise Men did. They didn't make their way to Jesus' stable and then hand out gifts to each other. "Here, Balthasar, you get the gold." "Merry Christmas, Gaspar, you can have the frankincense." No, they gave their gifts to a poor refugee family and for a child living in a wretched circumstance.

There have been others who exemplified the Christmas spirit.

For example, there really was a **Saint Nicolas**, who became known as Santa Clause. He was a Christian bishop of the Third Century. He was known for giving gifts to the poor, secretly leaving presents on the doorsteps of homes with children. In particular, Nicolas was known for leaving bags of gold at the homes of young girls who, if they didn't have a dowry, would end up in prostitution.

I chose this passage from **Titus** because the Christian, Titus, was known as a generous, Christmas-like person. The Apostle Paul mentions Titus nine times in his letters and each time, Paul is thanking Titus for his charitable work in helping those in need. Titus was the pastor of congregation in Crete, which would be like a pastor of any downtown church with great need and few resources. Cretan people were poor, uneducated and their skin was a different color, and yet, it was the Cretan church who helped the churches of the more Upper Class congregations, like the church in Corinth. You see, it is a nice thing when rich people help the poor; it's something else altogether when the poor help the rich. This was Titus.

When we think of the Wise Men, St. Nicolas and Titus, they seem to have the real meaning of Christmas in mind. But, when we watch all the commercials for Christmas, they seem to have a different purpose.

St. Nicolas – he didn't sneak in leave bags of gold on his own kid's beds. He went out and found young girls whose entire future was in jeopardy - and he saved them.

Maybe the real meaning of Christmas is in what Titus did. He didn't go shopping for the person who had everything. He rallied the Christians in Crete to help the Christians in Corinth, most likely helping people who didn't really like them much at all.

Maybe one way WE can re-claim Christmas this year is to define it according to **our** faith and **our** tradition. It is a good thing to extend love to the people we care about, to buy gifts for our family and our friends (and our pastor), but it might get closer to the meaning if we spend a little more on those in need and give more attention to those we normally ignore.

We define Christmas when we remember what the Wise Men did, what St. Nicolas did and what Titus did. They defined Christmas by that odd but beautiful tradition of giving that expects nothing in return. Which is, of course, all that God did when he sent the Christ Child into the world, to save us and bless us, now and forever.

TO GOD BE THE GLORY FOREVER AND EVER. AMEN.

Speaking Without Words
John 1: 1-18

When I was in high school, I remember having a copy of Judy Collins singing "Amazing Grace." Every night, I would listen to the song on my record player, over and over again, until finally the record gave out. I heard more snap, crack and pop than I did "amazing grace."

I thought I was odd, which I probably was, and just not for that reason. After I became a minister, I can't count how many times people wanted certain music played at their weddings or special songs at funerals. Because, just like it had been for me, the music had touched their souls. Hearing it again brought back all those memories of happier times and all the happiness of being with the person who was now gone.

Music has that power, doesn't it?

Most of us here can probably think of a song which makes us happy, or songs which make us feel sad. Music has an extraordinary power to touch us like nothing us. Music can heal and inspire. Music can comfort us when we are hurt and elevate us when we are down.

There is this one scene in the movie, "The Shawshank Redemption." We see a man wrongly imprisoned. He manages to get into the prison office. He finds a record: "The Marriage of Figaro" by Mozart. Suddenly he has a gleam in his eye. He puts on the record and places it next to the intercom. The next thing we hear is a soprano duet soaring over the entire prison. The prisoners all stop what they are doing to listen. They don't just listen. We see their heads turned up - as if they are being forced to think of heaven. Then the narrator said, "It was as if all the walls had disappeared and we were free." The scene ends when the guards kick in the door and break the record, but it is too late. He has given the prisoners something in those few minutes that no one can take away.

My first church was in a small town in rural Indiana. The population of the town was a little over a thousand. One Advent, a high school girl from our church, offered to sing. She was a music major at Indiana University. I had never heard her sing before so I didn't know what to expect. She got up and sang an Italian Christmas ballad. We were captivated. Like the prisoners listening to the music in the courtyard of Shawshank Prison, we had no idea what she was saying only that it was beautiful, and for a time, all our guilts and fears were relieved.

I think of this scene because of the passage we heard from the first chapter of John. "In the beginning was the Word, and the Word was with God, and the Word was God."

See, we probably don't realize it, but most biblical scholars believe that the first chapter of John was written to music. It was as if John knew that words alone could not express who Jesus was, so John set the story to a melody.

Even though the world repeatedly kicks down the door of faith, the music of Jesus endures. He is the light that shines in the darkness, and the darkness will never overcome it.

The powerful message of John is that Christ is the Word of God – even before Jesus was born, God was sending this music into the world.

The stories of the Bible, are stories of people who have heard the music of God and have done their best to share it with us.

People like Abraham and Sarah heard the music and shared it with us. Noah and Moses played their parts. David and Samuel, Deborah and Rahab, and endless prophets sang wonderful pieces for the world. They shared music that got us looking up and wondering about the divine and it was like the walls disappeared.

But it wasn't until Jesus that the words and the music and the beauty all came together in way that changed the world forever.

A friend of mine once said that when she was born again, she felt from that time on, Jesus was living in her. He was so real to her, that she would find herself singing – like Jesus helped her to hear a tune that had always been there, but now God was singing in her heart.

I thought that was a wonderful way of putting it.

She was able to hear a tune God was already singing. God is already in many places but people are not always listening."

All those years when Communism was suppressing the music of God in the former Soviet Union, God was still sending the notes out into their world. Thanks to the brave Russian Orthodox believers, the music was sung and people continued to hear about God's love and grace.

The message of Advent is that God is coming into the world, our world, our life. The music God started singing before the world was ever created became so real in Jesus, that no doubt, no discouragement, no deafening sound of despair will ever silence.

"Kingdom of God is at hand," said Jesus. God haunts our world with holiness. When Jesus was born to Mary and Joseph, the hidden song of God came screaming into our hurting, broken, and dark world, and nothing will silence God ever again – not for long.

Today, we give thanks for Christ who invites us to turn our heads up towards heaven, to hear and believe. Every now and then we will find reason to sing along.

TO GOD BE THE GLORY FOREVER AND EVER. AMEN.

CHRISTMAS EVE

Saying, 'Yes' to God
Luke 1: 38

We don't know what was going through Mary's mind as Gabriel spoke to her. According to Luke she was "perplexed" and she had to "ponder" what the Angel Gabriel just told her.

Can't help but think that's a bit of an understatement - telling this young, unmarried girl that she is going to have a child by God is like saying Hurricane Katrina was a summer breeze or that the Titanic sprung a leak. This was a big deal.

But, whatever she was thinking, it seems clear, Mary had to make a choice. The angel Gabriel may have been a long way from being a traveling salesman, but not too far from trying to sell Mary on the whole idea. Even the angel's greeting sounds like he is trying hard: "Greetings, favored one..."

Some imply that God already knew that Mary would say, YES, and so there was no real suspense. It was a done deal. Just like we know the Grinch will return the gifts to *Whoville*, Rudolph will save Christmas and Linus will tell us the real meaning of Christmas.

But, of course, we are all reading the story **after the fact**. At THAT moment - when Gabriel first appeared to Mary - maybe there was more suspense? Maybe Mary could have said, "No, thanks." Maybe the whole idea of having a baby out of wedlock before she was sixteen was not what she had planned. "Even if YOU say my child will be great, this is not what I planned!"

For all we know - for all anybody knows - God may have proposed the offer to others through the ages, but Mary was the first one to say, "Yes."

It was a brave thing she did.

Now, some say God's grace is so irresistible that Gabriel had only to ask and Mary had only to say, "Yes." *"Of course Mary would agree, who says, No, to God after all?"*

But, that's the thing – today, this very night, all we have to do is look around our world and realize we say, "No," to God all the time, don't we? We manage to find God VERY <u>resistible</u>.

As powerful as God may be, as convincing as God can be, as amazing as the grace of God **is** - we tend to be able to find a way to turn our back on God nonetheless, don't we? We do.

The truth is, we have an incredible ability to say, "No," to God. When we choose passing on gossipy stories about others instead pressing ourselves to accept the burden of self-examination, we are saying, "No" to God. When we embrace our pride rather than engage forgiveness, we are saying, "No" to God. When we habitually avoid houses of worship and distain talk of faith, we are saying, "No" to God. Anytime we turn away from the courage to use our life to bring a blessing into the world, we are saying "No," to God.

The truth is, we can say, "No," to God and we often do.

But, Mary said, "Yes."

Mary said, "Yes." And, what's more, Joseph said, "Yes" too. As much as Mary could have found her situation intolerable and Joseph could have found the situation unacceptable, but they both said, "Yes". And, that is why we are here tonight.

I have been thinking about other people who said, "Yes" to God. We are here tonight because we have said, "Yes" to God. We have a chance to say, "Yes" to God more often than we think of it. We say, "Yes" to God by expressing kindness in the face of rudeness. We say, "Yes" to God when we talk about our faith in a world which despises expressions of piety. Right now someone somewhere is saying, "Yes" to God. They are on their knees praying. They are caring for another person. They are refusing to give up hope or are sustaining the hope of another. All that is saying, "Yes" to God. Sometimes those moments are visible and truly amazing but sometimes they are quiet and only God knows the sweetness of the person's faith. But, people say, "Yes" to God even in the most unexpected places.

Back in 2000 I recall reading a book titled Three Cups of Tea. It told the story of a man who said, "Yes" to God. His name was, Greg Mortenson. He hadn't thought of himself as an especially religious man or even an especially good man. He had gone to Afghanistan to climb mountains. At some point he was separated from his group. Wandering, hungry and cold, he wandered into a village. The people there took him in and due to the leadership of the local Muslim Iman, they saved his life. Mortensen asked what he could do for them to repay them for their kindness? The elders and the Iman asked if he would please build a school so their girls could receive an education. Mortensen didn't feel he could do this. I mean they were half way around the world and who was he to accomplish such an incredible endeavor? Like Mary and Joseph, he didn't think God chose the right person. But, Mortensen said, "Yes" to God and by many acts of Providence, he has built hundreds of schools for girls in Afghanistan.

As we to hear politicians telling us how evil Muslims are, one of the stories Mortensen told still resonates with me. It was September 11, 2001. Mortensen was building a school in an Afghan village. When news of the tragedy from the terrorist attacks reached the village, the Muslim Iman and the elders of the village called all the people together. After everyone was together, the Iman held up his hand to ask for silence. Then they asked Mortensen to stand next to them. They said to him, "We are deeply sorry to hear about the death of so many people in your country." Then the Muslim Iman, asked all the people to pray. He led them in prayer asking for the mercies of God to be with the American people and to bring comfort - especially upon all the innocent families who are grieving.

The villagers said, "Yes" to God when they saved Mortsensen's life. Morstensen said, "Yes" to God when he went about building schools for the girls. The villagers, elders and Iman all said, "Yes" to God when they prayed for us that day.

Despite what we often hear, there are many righteous people around the world, in places we wouldn't expect, who are saying "Yes" to God. Many of these who are saying, "Yes" do so at great risk. Tonight we remember the shepherds said, "Yes" at great risk. The Wise Men said, "Yes" at great risk. Mary said, "Yes" at great risk. Joseph said, "Yes" at great risk. The question for tonight is, will we say, "Yes" to God even if it involves a great risk?

God brought good news of great joy for all people. Can we hear it? But, maybe most importantly, are we willing to share it?

TO GOD BE THE GLORY FOREVER AND EVER. AMEN.

EPIPHANY

Going Home by Another Way
Matthew 2: 1-18

I heard a story about an Abbot who was taking a young monk on a tour of a monastery to explain the work they do. The young monk asks, "So what do you do here?"

"We make copies of religious manuscripts." Said the Abbot.

"Do they copy from the originals?"

"O no," says the Abbot, "the originals are much too valuable. We keep those locked away. The brothers are making copies from copies."

The young monk asks, "But, isn't it possible someone wrote a word wrong and now you are just copying a mistake?"

"O no," said the Abbot, "we are much too careful for that."

But, the monk's question got the Abbot to thinking so he went into the vault to take a look at the originals. He was gone for a long time and the brothers began to worry about him, so they went to check on him. When they found him, he was bent over weeping. And all the brothers asked him, "What's wrong Abbot?" The Abbot said, "The word was **celebrate** not **celibate**." All this time copying the wrong word.

In this story from the gospel of Matthew, we get the sense that not only are Herod and the Magi reading different words, but they are reading from entirely different books. When Herod hears about the birth of the Christ Child, he is threatened and ends up killing all the innocent male children of Bethlehem. When the Magi hear about the Christ Child, they want to worship him. When they find him, they praise God for this good and beautiful Child. Two totally different responses to the same Child. One believes the Christ

Child is a terrible threat. The others believe the Christ Child is a holy blessing.

Maybe they are reading from two different books? Maybe, the truth is, we all read from different books? Perhaps the way we look at the book is different for each one of us?

All of us live out of a text that was formed while we were children. What got written into our personal text was what mother always told us or what father always did. Our personal text was written in the font of the culture we lived in.

One of my preaching professor's, Fred Craddock, told us a story about growing up in Alabama. One time when he was a teenager he was working on his uncle's farm bailing hay. His uncle had a Black man who worked on the farm with him. As they were bailing hay, the Black man said something to Craddock, he couldn't hear him and so he yelled back, *"What, sir?"* In an instant, the next thing he knew, his uncle had turned and slapped Craddock so hard it knocked him on the ground. As Craddock was on his back, trying to catch his breath. He looked up to see his uncle's face inches from his own, red with rage. His uncle said, *"If I ever hear you call him sir again, I'll whip you 'til you can't stand."* Craddock said, when you have that kind of experience etched into your book of life, it takes some time to edit it out.

Somewhere along the line, Herod had written in his book that if someone powerful is born, that person is a threat and should be killed. And, just the opposite, the Magi learned that the birth of child meant the presence of something good, and the birth of this particular child meant the presence of something especially good.

I suppose all of us would like to think we are more like the Magi: when we see something good and beautiful our reaction is to give thanks to God, and perhaps we do? But, do we ever find ourselves threatened by something good? If we do, it could be a little bit of the fearful Herod affecting our vision.

If we see someone driving a car that is nicer than ours, do we assume that person is shallow or do we think, "I bet that person is generous with the people they love"?

If we are at work and someone does a good job, do we assume they did it to make us look bad or do we assume they are simply hard workers?

If we are in high school and we see a pretty girl, do we assume she is stuck-up or do we assume she is a kind person?

If we see a pregnant unmarried teenage girl, do we assume she was just foolish or do we think of Mary, the mother of Jesus?

Can we think of times we felt threatened by something that perhaps was really good and beautiful?

Maybe there are good and beautiful things all around us - things from God - but we had so many pre-conceived notions written into our books, we were tempted to discard what was sacred?

Years ago I remember watching a television show that took place in a small town in the 1930's. It was during the rise of Nazism in Germany. In one episode they learned Hitler was burning books in Germany, so they decided to destroy all the German books they could find. In the process, they began to look on their German neighbors with suspicion.

As they gathered around the pile of books, one of the characters tried to stop them, insisting that burning books and treating their German neighbors poorly was acting like Hitler. They were about to push him aside and light the books when he looks down and he picks up one of the German books. He asks one of the German neighbors standing off to the side, if she would read from the book. At first she reads in *German*. Then, he asked her to read it in English. She said, **"In the beginning, God created the heavens and the earth..."**

Suddenly, they saw things differently. They realized there was something sacred where they had only seen something fearful.

Now they were seeing the world as the Magi did. They turned apologized to their neighbors who picked up their books and they all went home by another way.

Sometimes there is goodness and beauty and we can miss it if we are not looking for it.

Herod didn't realize that Jesus came to save him. All he saw was a threat. But the wise men saw the truth. Jesus was goodness and beauty that had come to save the world.

All of us come in here with our own texts. Some of our texts have words of grace and love. Some are etched with notions better left edited out. Jesus came so we could see the world as he does.

We don't always do what Jesus would do, but we might still ask ourselves, what would Jesus see right now, if he were here?

Our hope is to go home using the Bible as our text, reading the book which tells us about and love and forgiveness. We can set down the book of fear and pick up the book which teaches us not to fear. We can go home another way, reading a different text, following a hopeful star that will lead us to place so much better from whence we came.

TO GOD BE THE GLORY FOREVER AND EVER. AMEN.

VALENTINES' DAY

Two Loves, One God
Song of Solomon 2: 10-14; John 15: 9-13

This Song of Solomon passage is very fitting for Valentine's Day, but it's also very embarrassing. Maybe ideal for a couple celebrating an anniversary or wedding, but somehow it feels out of place in worship. We might even blush while reading it.

There's a Peanut's cartoon where Lucy is leaning over Schroeder's piano and she says, "If you don't tell me you love me, I'll hold my breath until I pass out." Schroeder says, "Did you know that breath holding is a sign of a metabolic disorder? You might have a vitamin B-6 deficiency. You might consider eating more bananas. Avocados and beef liver might help." Lucy says, "Wouldn't you know it. I ask for love and I get beef liver."

When we hear the two passages today it's hard to think of two kinds of love which could be farther apart. The Song of Solomon over here and the Gospel of John over here. The one love wanting to take and hold and the other love wanting to sacrifice and give. Two loves: Yet One God who made them all.

The first love is found in the Song of Solomon which is a little book in the Bible that most of us know nothing about. It may show up in the lectionary, but ministers mostly avoid it. We may hear it at weddings and even then we tend to smirk. We don't refer to it much because there doesn't seem to anything spiritual about it. The book is about the courtship between a man and a woman. It's kind of like one of those romance novels we see at the drug store where on the cover there is almost always a picture of a man (with a torn shirt) carrying a woman somewhere - which is obviously a sign of love. Why else would he do that?

"Arise, my love, and come away for your voice is sweet and your face is lovely." Sounds like a love letter we might have written when we were dating but would deny if our children happened to find it.

Supposedly, the Song of Solomon was penned by King Solomon himself, whom tradition suggests was very wise. However, the same tradition says he had 700 wives. Not sure of the wisdom there, but I guess it is safe to say he would have had practice writing love letters, if not apologies.

"Arise, my love, my fair one, and come away," says the man to the woman. "For the winter is over and the spring is here." As we all know, anytime we are in love, it is spring. That is the one kind of love.

Just opposite the Song of Solomon is the Gospel of John. It is a whole different love. Jesus is preparing to leave his disciples. It is a somber moment. Sad and quiet. Just imagine saying good-bye to the people we love?

What's interesting is Jesus doesn't say anything churchy; he doesn't give them a list of do's and don'ts. Instead, I think he said what any of us would say. He tells them that he loves them and he wants them to go on loving: "love one another as I have loved you."

In one way they are the words of a man, a human being, like any of us, the kind of thing we hope we would be able to say to people we loved. But, there is something divine going on too. Behind the shadow Jesus's words is the presence of God. There is something about this love which is not just human. It's a rare love when we are willing to put another's needs before our own. That is the other kind of love.

So, there we have it. Two loves. Two very different kinds of love. One love is desiring, reaching out, grasping for more. The other love is sacrificial, letting go, seeking to give. The first love is the kind of love we warn our children about. "Don't be fooled," we say. The other love is the kind of love we hope they will find some day: a "love which bears through all things, endures all things, a love which never ends."

On the surface they don't seem to fit together at all and yet, here they are snug in the Bible like two birds in a nest, which tells us that although they may be different, they are from the same God. They may not fit together and, yet, there they are. Maybe they are both here because there is really only one love, really, just like there is only one God. Ice cream is ice cream, it may come in your run-of-the-mill vanilla or your exotic rocky road with strawberry bits, but it all comes from milk. Well, all our loves, no matter how plain or how deep, all come from God. One love. One God. One source. Different flavors.

Whatever kind of love we have…whether it is the steamy courtship love or the tender parental love or the saintly giving love, they are all from God and all of them say something about God and they say something about what God hopes for us.

And there is something really radical to think about: maybe God's love is passionate, reaching out and yearning just like our human love can be? Maybe the Song of Solomon says something about the aching love God for us? God yearns for love like we sometimes yearn for one another?

In the book of the prophet, Hosea, God sounds like a lover who has been rejected by her beloved, and is pleading for him to come back again. Listen to what God says in the Book of Hosea: "The more I called to Israel, the more they turned away from me…I drew him to me. I picked them up and held them to my cheek…The Lord says, 'I will bring my people back to me. I will love them with all my heart.'" (Hosea 11; 14:4)

You see, God has that same kind of restlessness for us as we do for each other. This embarrassing, passionate, hungry, human love we have for one another is not a distortion of God's love, but just another a reflection, just another sweet flavor.

Think about this. When Jesus went off to pray, he wasn't just going off to be alone, Jesus was going off to listen for the One Voice he needed to hear: "Arise, my beloved, come with me." So, if we listen to the words in between the words in the Song of Solomon, what we can hear, if we listen, is an invitation from God to come away for a while.

Someone once said:

> To be in love with someone is to find your whole being tied up with the beloved...You can no more forget the one you love than you could forget your own name...You want to share yourself, all of yourself with your beloved...Separation is a restless sorrow. In reunion the world seems complete. Those who are caught up in such love for another can catch a fragmentary, fleeting glimpse of the love God has for [us].
>
> (Christian Century: 8/10/94)

Whenever we find love, we find something of God. Wherever we find the yearning emptiness for our beloved, what we are **truly** finding is our yearning emptiness for God. And, the truth is, brothers and sisters, the more we can fill that emptiness with God, the more we can love those whom are dear to us. Hear the word of the Lord: "Arise, my love, my fair one, and come away."

"...O Lord, beneath our hunger for one another lies a deeper hunger yet, a deeper emptiness which finally only you can fill. Open our hearts to the knowledge that we can be fully each other's only when we are fully yours."[1]

TO GOD BE THE GLORY FOREVER AND EVER. AMEN.

---

[1] From Frederick Buechner in *The Hungering Dark*, p. 88.

LENT

The Last Temptation of Christ
Matthew 4: 1-11

When the devil had finished all this tempting, he left him until an opportune time. Luke 4:13

I heard a story about a man who goes to his priest for Confession. He says to the priest, "Father, I have sinned. I work for a lumber yard and over the years I stole enough lumber to build myself a house. But, I didn't stop there. I stole enough wood to build a home for each of my children." "My goodness," says the priest, "these are serious sins. Have you considered a penitential retreat?" "No, Father, I have not seen one of those, but if you give me the plans I think I know where I can get the lumber."

When most of us think of temptations, we think of things which are either bad for us or simply just bad, right? Too much food, too much self-pity, too much inappropriate intimacy. But, the truth is few people set out to do evil.

I had an uncle who said, "I have no problem choosing between good and evil. My problem is choosing between two goods." Most of us want something good, perhaps something very good, the problem is we don't realize *what* we are being tempted to sacrifice to get this good thing.

See, the real problem with temptations is they can all *seem* OK. Temptation to do evil happens when we take something good in itself and we sacrifice something more good to get it.

In the silly story, having a home or building home for our child are good things, but if this means sacrificing honesty to get them, they become evil. In more serious temptations, people still have good intentions but the Ends do not justify the Means.

In the year 1097, the Christians of Europe set out on their first Crusade. They wanted to assist God in restoring the Holy Land as preparation for the Kingdom of God: A good thing, right? After all shouldn't we do all we can to assist God and prepare the Kingdom of Heaven? Doesn't the Bible say, "Every knee shall bow and every tongue confess Jesus Christ as Lord and Savior"? *"Well, then,"* they thought, *"we will make it our calling to make sure people's knees are bowed and their tongues are confessing Christ as Lord."* So, the Knights of the Cross raced to the Holy Land cleansing the land of anyone who did not confess Christ as Lord. One of their stops was the Turkish city of Nicea. The people there had dark skin and didn't say, "Jesus Christ is Lord." So, the Crusaders killed every man, woman and child - in order to prepare for the Kingdom of Heaven.

It was only after the last cries of their victims died down that the Crusaders had an unsettling revelation. They turned the bodies over to find the dead were wearing crosses around their necks. They had just slaughtered a community of Christians. The Crusaders hadn't stopped to consider that Christ may have already been there before them. Just because the people looked different and spoke different, did not mean they also were not preparing for the Kingdom of God in their own way.

In our own nation, we have made our own mistakes in seeking the good.

Some leaders have advocated torture – something we condemn when other nations do it – but, it would seem, some leaders in our country imply torture is OK if done for the ***right*** reason. So it goes - Too often temptation to do evil will be couched in an attempt to do something good.

Now, of course, WE – in this room - have no intention of killing anyone for a good reason, no matter how good. Our temptations will be subtle, won't they? Our temptations will likely be more like the Seven Deadly Sins: pride, anger, envy, lust… We are not tempted to kill, but tempted to covet, yes. Not always easy to choose the "good" choices.

We may believe honesty is good and we want to resist the temptation to lie. But, if our wife asks us, "Do I look fat in this?" What should we say? Or, for that matter, if our husband says, "I am a great dancer, aren't I dear?" What should the wife say?

Temptation is always couched in good. So, we will have to ask ourselves, "By making this choice are we sacrificing a greater good?" There is seldom an easy answer. If it was easy, it would not be tempting.

Which brings us to Jesus today.

When we read the temptations Satan gave Jesus we think to ourselves, "Well, those were easy choices, not much temptation there: of course, no one should test the Lord, and of course, we should not worship anybody but God." But, within all these temptations is something very good, which is why the choice was harder than we realized.

In the first temptation, Jesus is hungry – he has fasted for 40 days. Is it bad to be hungry or want food? Of course not. In fact, later on Jesus would make sure hungry people had more than enough food. He fed 5,000 people. Would it have been wrong to feed himself?

In the second temptation, Satan reminds Jesus - by quoting Psalm 91, no less - that the righteous will not come to harm. We were taught that at some point, weren't we? Do the right thing and God will be with us. We learned that in Sunday School.

In the final temptation, Satan offers to let Jesus rule the world. And isn't that exactly what we Christians want? Isn't that what we work for – a world where Jesus is King and the Voice of Christ is heard over all the voices?

All three of these temptations are good in themselves: food, protection, a Christ-led world.

But, at what cost?

This was the question for Jesus and it is often the question for us.

What are we sacrificing to get the good thing we want?

I recall a poem which seems to go to the heart of it all:

> If I could give my right, I'd say, "Take it all away."
> If I could give my left, I'd gladly do the same.
> For the price of happiness is never too high,
> The cost of life and liberty n'er too steep.
> Until after all tis said and done
> and realize
>   my soul I gave for play.

Jesus saw the danger. The temptation to serve Satan often comes cloaked in good choices.

Jesus knew this.

One of the best books on the life of Christ was written by Nikos Kazantzakis. The book is titled, *The Last Temptation of Christ*. As we read the book we see the struggle of the human Jesus trying to accept his divine call. He slowly but surely realizes who he is and what he is supposed to do. Ultimately, in the final chapter, we see the last temptation of Christ played out.

The scene is the cross. Jesus is suffering, betrayed by his friends, hung between the two thieves, and a crown of thorns on his head. He hears someone say to him, "If you really are the Messiah, call down the angels so they will lift you up from the cross!" Then, Jesus calls the angels. They miraculously take him down. They immediately cure him of his injuries. The Jewish leaders are silenced and the Romans do not know what to make of it, so they set him free. Jesus goes on to live a normal life. He and Mary Magdalene set up house. They have children. He takes on the family carpentry business. All is well.

Then, as he nears the end of this life, Jesus is sitting on his porch, watching the sun go down and listening to his children. Suddenly from up the road he sees a figure marching towards him. Kicking up dust, we see "a short, bald, wild-eyed man with power in his stride and God on his breath." It is the Apostle Paul.

Paul comes up to Jesus. Paul is furious. He yells at Jesus, "What have done?" "You have given it all away?! You have sacrificed the world for the sake of your own comfort?!" Paul is then joined by the disciples, by Peter and John and Mark and all the rest. Their disappointment is like fire burning his skin. They all accuse Jesus of being a coward.

Jesus realizes they are right. He has been a coward – he chooses a normal life. He by coming down off the cross, he chooses the easy way. He wanted to be safe and content – like many of us just want to be safe and content – but in choosing what we so often choose, Jesus was a coward. They rail at him and walk away in disgust. As the story winds down, Jesus is shivering with despair because not only do Paul and the Apostles reject him, but so does God.

Then, just as Jesus is about to give to up hope, something happens. This is how Kazantzakis ends his book:

> He felt terrible pains in his hands and feet and heart...His head quivered. Suddenly he remembered where he was, who he was and why he felt pain. A wild, indomitable joy took possession of him. No, no he was not a coward, a deserter, a traitor. No, he was nailed to the cross. He had stood his ground to the very end; he has kept his word. The moment he had cried, "ELOI, ELOI" he had fainted, Temptation had captured him for split second and led him astray. The joys, marriages and children were lies; the decrepit, degraded old men who shouted, "coward, deserter, traitor" at him were lies. All - all were illusions sent by the Devil. His disciples were alive and thriving. They had gone over sea and land were proclaiming the Good News. Everything had turned out as it should, glory be to God!
>
> He uttered a triumphant cry: "IT IS ACCOMPLISHED!"
>
> And it was as though he had said, "Everything has begun."

Jesus resisted the temptation to just live a normal and safe life. He didn't just choose what was good. He chose what was better.

Maybe living a safe, content and comfortable life is not what God intends for us? Maybe God wants us to give up being safe and content and comfortable for a greater work of God?

May the Spirit which inspired Jesus, be the same Spirit which guides us. May God help us choose the better over the good.

TO GOD BE THE GLORY FOREVER AND EVER. AMEN.

PALM SUNDAY

Palm Sunday Lament
Matthew 21: 1-11

Probably the hardest part of Palm Sunday is we know what's going to happen. What's more, we can't help but wish it wouldn't happen the way it does. It's like watching those documentaries on the life of Lincoln, there's this aching hope someone will stop John Wilkes Booth. We wish the crowds that cheer Jesus on Sunday will protect him on Friday. We wish the Sanhedrin would fall down on their knees in worship. We wish the disciples would dig deep and find courage. We wish Pilate would have had a clue. But, of course, that isn't what happens. Each year the same people disappoint us. So, the story ends the same. Jesus came to rescue sinners, but the sinners betray him. On Palm Sunday, we know what's going to happen and that's probably the hardest part.

I suppose what is equally disturbing is that we know that we are not that unlike the crowd. Maybe we wouldn't have betrayed him or been one of those who yelled, "Crucify him!" But, just like them, we are selfish and scared and sometimes sin is bigger than simple choices. From the Japanese Internment Camps of WWII, segregating Black members to church balconies, or the treatment of prisoners at Abu Grade – all these things much bigger than us and yet the blood still seems to be on our hands - even if we did nothing. We sin, or take part in sin, and we hardly even know it. Except with Palm Sunday, we see it coming.

So, the question is, "Why do we bother telling this Palm Sunday story over and over again when we already know they are not going to get it? And why bother, when we know WE aren't going to get it right either?" We are going to stumble into sin and find ourselves in the same hole again just as they did. "Why do we keep telling the Palm Sunday story if we know what they did and what we do?"

Well, I suppose, the reason we keep telling the story is because the story isn't about the crowds or us. It's about Jesus. Maybe we waver, maybe the crowds wavered, maybe the disciples and the Sanhedrin wavered, but Passion Week is the story of a man who did not waver. As T. S. Elliott once wrote, "Christ is the still center in a revolving world." That's why we retell the story. To remind us on how when everybody else was getting it wrong, Jesus showed us how to get it right.

When we hear the story, one thing is clear from the very beginning, Jesus is in charge. Jesus sends two disciples into town (He doesn't ask for volunteers). He says, "You two, go!" Then he tells them exactly what to do. He tells them to bring him a donkey and a colt, and if anyone questions them about them, he tells them exactly what to say. We often think that Jesus' plans were somehow spoiled by the fickleness of the crowds: if they hadn't turned on him, things would have turned out OK. If the disciples had been brave, or if Pilate would have had some integrity, then the entrance into Jerusalem wouldn't have been a failure. But, I believe what Matthew is telling us is the crowds, the disciples, the Sanhedrin, even Pilate himself, had little to do with what was going on. In one of the gospel recollections it said, "When Jesus came into Jerusalem and the crowds were cheering him, the Pharisees told Jesus to shush the crowds, remember what Jesus said? "I tell you, if these were silent, the very stones would cry out." Even if there were no crowds, the stones would be sufficient. He hardly needs the crowds to do what needs to be done. Granted, they showed a self-interest not too unlike our own. But, in the most important way, the Passion story has nothing to do with them. They might as well be stones along the road.

Some people say that Jesus HAD to die on the cross to free us from sin. But it seems to make more sense to say that it was inevitable that Jesus died on the cross and Jesus knew that. Jesus knew wherever there is love, there is sacrifice and the greater the love, the greater will be the sacrifice. We know it is true in our own lives. The more love we have for our children or our beloved or for our friend, the more likely that love, if it is real, will demand a sacrifice. So, as someone once said, *it wasn't nails that held Jesus to the cross, it was love.* Even if there had been no nails at all, love would have held him fast to the cross.

When I was in seminary I heard this parable to try to explain how Jesus died for our sins. The parable goes like this. There was once a railroad drawbridge operator who had a son. One day the drawbridge was up and the operator saw that a train was coming. Just as he was about the lower the bridge, he noticed his young son was down below playing on the gears of the drawbridge. If he lowered the bridge, he would kill his son, but, if he didn't lower the bridge, the people on the train would die. He had to make a choice, so he lowered the bridge, sacrificing his son, to save the people on the train.

The parable was supposed to explain how God sacrificed Jesus to save us. But I tell you what, when I heard the story it didn't help me at all. I had two little girls at the time and a third one on the way, the idea of killing them to save others made no sense to me! Is this what God did? Did God kill his own child to save us? This really confused me. So, I talked to a seminary professor and asked, "What kind of father would sacrifice his son?"

That's when the professor helped me understand. It was not only the human Jesus who died on the cross, it was God who died on the cross. So, a better use of the parable would have gone this way: the drawbridge operator, seeing his son on the gears, set the bridge to come down, but somehow jumped out of the window pushing his son to safety and gave his own life, to save both his son and the people on the train. God didn't kill anyone. God was willing to die for us.

We retell this story to remember that even when everybody else was getting it wrong, Jesus got it right. He refused to give up on love to very end.

So, as we begin this Holy Week, knowing how it will end, we also know the good news. That even if we do fail him, he showed us he would not fail us. The fact that things turned sour, as they often do, does not change the fact that God, didn't hold that against us.

Even if we are going to repeat some of the same mistakes, in the end, our lack of bravery will not stop God.

Perhaps the bravery of Jesus will inspire us to be brave?

TO GOD BE THE GLORY FOREVER AND EVER. AMEN.

MAUNDY THURSDAY

I Love You. Eat.
John 16: 16-24; John 17: 20- 26

Whenever we read an obituary, it usually starts with when and where a person was born, who their parents were. Then the obituary goes on to mention, siblings, spouse and then the children, this is usually followed by accomplishments - all of this written in somewhat chronological order. They write as if the most important things are what happened first. I guess you could say the day of our birth is significant, but if you think about it, it might be more appropriate to write an obituary beginning with the end of a person's life. Because it is at the end of a life that we can really see the events that were significant. We usually don't realize the moments that changed our life until after they are over. It is often in looking back that the oddly shaped pieces of our life fit together like a jigsaw puzzle.

You don't have to be a biblical scholar to see that's how the Bible was written. Nothing in the Bible was written as the event occurred, as if the writers were on-the-scene reporters, rather, later, after the fact, maybe even years later, as the believers talked, they began to understand and pull things together.

That was especially true with Jesus. Many places in the Bible, the writers point out that the disciples had no idea what Jesus was talking about at the time - it was only until much later that it made sense. They couldn't comprehend him or what he was saying all at once; they couldn't understand his message nor accept the love offered, at least not at the moment. It was only when he was gone that they realized who he was and what he meant to them.

What a person does and says at the end of their life, speaks volumes about how they lived their life. The Bible is clear that Jesus knew his time was near. He knew he would be leaving this life at any time. Maybe it is fairly important to consider what he did before he left.

He prayed that his disciples would not be left alone. He prayed that the Holy Spirit would comfort and strengthen them. He prayed that they would get along together and watch over each other. He prayed that they would come to be close with God as he was close with God. He washed their feet. He sat down with them and had a meal, saying he hoped this special meal would always remind them of his special love for them. Of all the things he could have prayed for and of all the things he could have done, even from the cross, his last words, his last actions, were those of compassion for the people he loved. When looking down from the cross, he saw his mother, distraught with tears, and he saw his disciple, John, standing next to her. He said to her, "Mother, behold your son." And to John he said, "Here is your mother." (John 19:25-27) His last action was to make sure someone took care of his mother.

A few years ago I officiated at a funeral of a man who had died of cancer. He had an awful form of stomach cancer. He couldn't eat. All his food was feed intravenously. Consequently, his wife had problems eating. She couldn't bring herself to sit down to a meal knowing her husband was going without. He didn't complain about his problem, but she just couldn't eat. So, while he was dying, in some sense, they were both dying.

What struck me as especially powerful however, is what happened shortly before the man died. The woman said to me, "His last words to me were, 'I love you. Eat.'" I did not know that man very well, but I do know that what a person does at the end of their life speaks volumes about how a person lived their life. Those words, his last actions and last words were expressions of love.

In some ways, his last words were reminiscent of Christ, because that's kind of what Jesus said to us, "I love you. Eat." He wants us to eat – together -and be nourished by his Spirit - together. Jesus isn't here in body, of course, he is waiting for us. He says he won't eat and drink until we can all be together in the kingdom. Like a grandmother who insists everybody must be at the table before we start to eat, Christ has set the table and is eagerly waiting for all of us to make it HOME. We share this meal in the Spirit of Christ, looking forward to the day we will share it with him and with all those beloved of God. It's so important that we be there with him, that he isn't going to start without us. He wants us to start getting ready by eating this meal together. These are the appetizers. The *hor d'oeuvres* of the Kingdom.

The good news is that man with the cancer is enjoying a meal with Christ, far better than anything we could whip up. He is full. As we look at the end of Jesus' life, we realize how important it is that we have this meal. "I love you, Eat." He said. Eat well, remembering that even our hunger for food is just a reflection of our hunger for God and in the kingdom we will all be satisfied.

TO GOD BE THE GLORY FOREVER AND EVER. AMEN.

EASTER

Running to The Tomb
John 20: 1-18

We often think of Spring and Easter as going together, don't we? Spring is about things which *appear* dead coming to life: brown ground turning green, buds appearing on trees, daffodils miraculously shooting up from the ground. We see all this and we think of Easter in kind of the same way. But, the truth is, they don't go together, do they? I mean, they are not the same thing.

Spring is natural. We expect it. Even after a stubborn winter, we know spring will win out. However, resurrections are not something we expect. There is nothing natural about it. The truth is, when people die, they go away. They don't come back next year at the same time. I remember a woman once telling me about how when she was little, she believed if she planted chicken bones she could grow chickens. Her four-year old logic was flawless. She thought: **"We plant corn to get corn. We plant beans to get beans. Why can't we plant chicken bones to get chickens?"** Even if they do happen at the same time, we know spring and Easter are different.

Of course, in the Gospel of John, Mary didn't have any illusions that first Easter morning. She wasn't thinking about a Jesus being raised from the dead on her way to the grave. No thoughts of how a tomb is like a cocoon and Jesus is like a butterfly. The other gospels talk about the women coming to prepare the body for burial, but according to John, Mary came too late to even see the body. Jesus was already buried. She missed the wake, the funeral and the grave side. She comes to the grave alone.

I suppose she went to the grave for the same reasons any of us go to graves. Maybe she went to confirm the reality of it, to allow it to sink in. Maybe to say a few things she never said to him while he was alive. But one thing for certain, she didn't go expecting a conversation, did she? Not surprising she didn't even recognize Jesus at first. I mean who would, right? It wasn't until he actually said her name, "Mary," only then that she recognized him.

Mary had no illusions that first Easter.

That's the difference, we celebrate this morning. Spring is about the **natural** things we expect: daffodils, Mother's Day, graduation from high school, Easter is about the **supernatural** things God does.

I want you to notice something interesting about the story this morning. When Mary and the disciples heard the tomb was empty, they did something a little odd. When they heard the tomb was empty, they **ran** to get there. Think about it. Who runs to a grave? What's the hurry? The tomb isn't going anywhere. Why bother running if they knew it was all mistake? They acted like people who suspected something unexpected had happened.

Maybe they ran because they wanted to see the empty tomb for themselves? Maybe they were confused. Maybe they were angry because someone had stolen the body and desecrated the tomb? But, maybe they were running because they believed something good had happened?

I'm sure, the overriding feelings Mary and the others had running to the tomb, were disbelief and worry - but, perhaps mixed in with all that, there was something else. There was just enough faith to believe that Jesus was alive after all?

And so they ran to the tomb. There's no reason to run to a tomb. It will be there tomorrow. But they ran. They ran because, **although the tomb may be there tomorrow, maybe HE wouldn't be there tomorrow?** They ran to the tomb.

Most of us are here today because at one time or another, God spoke OUR name when we least expected it. What I mean is we are here, either because we know we have been touched by God or because we want to be touched by God, and that is why we are here. There are these hopeless moments which suddenly come alive with hope. When that happens, it is just one more proof of God in the world.

One story came out of the national news awhile back. **TIME** magazine told the story of what happened when Ashley Smith stepped out of her house at 2:00 a.m. because she couldn't sleep. As she was walking, suddenly she met Brian Nichols. The day before, Nichols, had stepped into a courthouse shot and killed several people where he was being arraigned on rape charges. Nichols took her to her apartment where he tied her up and put her in her bathtub. He said he wouldn't hurt her if she just did what he said.

What would we do in that situation? Cry? Panic? Beg?

Instead, Smith talked to him, not as a monster (though in many ways, he was), she talked to him as a human being. She calmly told him the story of her life. Her husband had been stabbed in a fight and had died in her arms. She developed a drug habit and had been ticketed for speeding and drunk driving. Eventually she was arrested for assault. With her life such a mess, she eventually gave up custody of her daughter to her aunt. With her own life barely afloat she was facing a man whose life seemed to be sinking fast.

What happened next is what the **TIME** author said verged on the incredible. Smith had been reading The Purpose Driven Life by the Christian author, Rick Warren. The book's premise is that God is always working in our lives to guide us towards grace - even at those moments when we are convinced grace has forgotten us. She had just finished chapter 33 which was about *serving others*. That night she read what Warren wrote. He said "...great opportunities to serve never last long. You may only get one chance to serve a person, so take advantage of the moment." Smith saw this as her moment to make a difference. She talked to Nichols some more. He eventually let her out of the tub. She told him more about her life and her brokenness. She cooked him breakfast and eventually convinced him to turn himself in. Nichols said afterwards that it was like he was speaking to an angel sent to him from God.

Neither one of these people are saints but as the **TIME** author wrote, "Grace arrives unannounced, in lives that least expect it or deserve it."

The Easter message is that God works with the crooked lumber of human failure to build altars of grace. God uses the crooked lumber of Ashley Smith's life, to bring about a turn of grace. She survived and who knows how many other people she saved?

We are resurrection people. Because of Easter, we can have hope.

Maybe there is something in our lives this morning that needs a resurrection? Maybe we are not here this morning by accident. We may be sure there is no hope, but there is hope. We could be wrong about things being hopeless. Who would have thought that Ashley Smith - with her life teetering near shambles - could ever have been a messenger of hope? But she was. She did what she felt God was calling her to do and something like a miracle happened.

Resurrection is not something that happens naturally, but it does happen. Somehow, God raises up good things where we are sure there is no chance good can happen. The disciples ran to the tomb because although it wasn't natural and although it wasn't spring, there was something that told them to run. May we find ourselves walking fast to church on Sunday, so we can be sure to be here when Jesus calls our name.

TO GOD BE THE GLORY. FOREVER AND EVER. AMEN.

PENTECOST SUNDAY

How Will We Speak?
Acts 2: 1-8; Genesis 11: 1-9

It would be good if we all spoke the same language, wouldn't it? There would be a few less problems in the world if we all used the same words. At least we might have a few more opportunities.

When I was a freshman in high school I had just moved from Chicago to a little rural town in the state of Indiana. I spoke different than they and visa-versa. There was a girl who I thought was just beautiful: Maureen Sharp. I wanted to ask Maureen out for a date, but I was too shy, so instead I did what most kids do at that age, I asked her cousin, Laurie, if she would ask Maureen if she liked me and if she would go out with me. Well, the next day, I saw Laurie. She said, "Well, Melty (my nick-name), you lucked out." And I said, "Oh, really. Ok." and I walked away sad. See I thought that when I person had "lucked out," that was like saying, "You're out of luck." I thought she was telling me that Maureen wasn't interested in going out with me, so I never asked her. It was a language problem. You should have seen me years later when I realized "lucked out" meant we are so lucky we used up all our luck. I was married with three daughters when someone said "lucked out" and I said, "What did you say?" and then I understood. "Oh no! I could have gone out with Maureen Sharp!" Having one language would have been nice that in 1974. At least it would have been good for me.

Yet, according to our first scripture today – the story of the Tower of Babel - God seems opposed to having the same language. In Genesis 11:6, God says in a concerned voice, "Behold, they are one people, and they have all one language; and this is only the beginning of what they will do; and nothing will be impossible for them. Come let us go down, and there confuse their language, that they may not understand one another's speech." And that's what

God did. And ever since, we have been misunderstanding each other, hiring translators, missing all kinds of potential dates.

Why would God do this to us? What's wrong with everyone speaking the same language? What's wrong with people cooperating for a change? Most of us are weary of political parties where they only thing they really know is the other side is wrong. What's wrong with humanity working together so that "nothing that they propose will be impossible for them"?

God sounds clearly concerned and we are clearly confused.

But, if we think about it, we know there is a side to unity which isn't all that good, isn't there? There is a kind of unity which forces conformity. Calvin and Hobbes is a newspaper cartoon. Calvin is the precocious little boy and Hobbes is his stuffed tiger alter ego. At one point Calvin says to Hobbes, "I could solve all the disagreements in the world, if people would just do what I say."

There is the mob-mentality kind of unity, where people in a group can lose their sense of morality and do things as a group that they would never do as individuals.

There is an oppressive unity. When we look back, we know some of the greatest tyrants in history wanted uniformity of language and belief. Dissentions were unwelcome and when these people talked about unity what they were really saying is we want to rid ourselves of all the people who are different from us. Then we'll have unity. We want to build walls. Circumvent dissention, pigeon-hole the unique and oppress variety. The tyrants often want to keep out the people who are different and diminish those who disagree.

And so, maybe here is where we can begin to understand God's concern in Genesis. God says, "If they keep this up, there will be nothing they won't stop at doing." "They will do anything." God has reason to be concerned. We know sometimes unity means is everybody else has to think like us, behave like us, believe like us. This is not really the unity God wants nor do we.

But, there is a unity we all long for. There is a kind of unity which comes being glad when someone has something new to offer and something different to say. You have probably heard the saying, "In heaven we will find all the people we love"? But, I heard someone say it in a way which really made me think. Maybe instead of saying, "In heaven we will find all the people we love, we could say, **"In heaven we will love all the people we find."** That is heaven.

You see, when we look around the world it should be obvious that God created us diverse. God enjoys the sound of different voices and different languages - for God it is the way it should be.

Where would be the beauty in a musical composition with every one playing the same note? Where would be the beauty in a Van Gogh with no yellow, red and greens? What would be use of marriage if there was no ying for our yang?

The beauty is not in the sameness we enjoy but in the salve we provide.

Heaven on earth is when we can learn to love the other.

I want you to notice something today. Take a look at the passage from Genesis and the passage from Acts. Notice in Genesis 11:1 - in the story of the Tower of Babel, all the people **spoke the same language**. Everybody used the same words - and there was something bad about this. But, notice in Acts 2: 6. Jesus has just left the room. He has left them to go heaven, but he promises to send a Spirit, a Comforter, an Advocate, to help them. What's interesting in the story of the first Pentecost – after Jesus leaves – he sends the Holy Spirit which allowed the disciples to **speak in different languages** - the opposite of the story of the Tower of Babel when the people were all **speaking the same language.** It is a subtle difference but it's an extraordinary difference. In the first story, left to ourselves, all possible differences are erased and we become a desert of sameness. In the second story, when God comes near, God doesn't make us the same, God doesn't say we must conform, bend or break, adopt or leave, congeal or be poured down the drain. What God does is make us different, say that is good and then helps us to communicate with each other.

The Holy Spirit doesn't take away our differences; the Holy Spirit helps us hear despite our differences. Anyone who has lived any time at all knows that the real miracle happens when we are able to understand each other - we all have the same cries for forgiveness, longing for love, hunger for God and fear of aloneness. Pentecost turned around Babel: now we can understand each other.

This is the kind of unity brings delight to the heart of God. It is a unity that comes from mutual respect. This is the kind of Pentecost unity we celebrate and makes us stronger and better.

Today we confirmed several young people into our church: Kyle, Morgan, Will, Athena, Matthew, Kevin, Jake, and Matthew. Our joy comes because we believe each one of them brings something new to us. With each of them, we think of a new pane of color added to a stained glass window. Through each one we hope to see a new shade of grace and experience a new hue of holiness.

Our prayer is the Holy Spirit will help us understand one another. The presence of God is measured in the level of respect we practice and the depth of tolerance we bear for one another.

May God be so kind as to help us to hear and speak to one another as if we are talking with Christ himself. If we can speak to each other in this way, the Spirit of God is not far off. That is a language we can all hear.

TO GOD BE THE GLORY FOREVER AND EVER. AMEN

CHRIST OUR KING SUNDAY

Taraxacum asteracea
John 12: 9-19

There is a flower we often see in the spring. Its Latin name is ***Taraxacum asteracea***. It's a beautiful name really: *taraxacum asteracea*. The flower is extremely hardy. They resist disease, bugs, heat, cold, wind, rain - even human beings. It is almost impossible to kill them. We can mow over them. We can pull them up. It doesn't matter. What's more the leaves are a good source of vitamin A and C; they are high in iron. They make salads, tea and wine. What's really neat is the flowers perform magic: when they bloom they turn into hundreds of little parachute seeds that start new plants everywhere. Do you know what flower I am talking about? Anyone? A more common name for *taraxacum asteracea* is the *dandelion*, which comes from Latin meaning, "tooth of the lion." Dandelions are king of the flowers, actually they are the king of the weeds.

But, there is a problem with *taraxacum asteracea*. There's a problem. The problem is that they grow wherever they want to. They have a mind of their own. They grow wherever they want.

I got to thinking about this and I realized that if dandelions didn't grow so well on their own - I mean if they were fragile, delicate flowers - we would probably buy expense pot and grow them in our homes. If we happened to find one in our yard, we'd call our friends over and say, "Hey, look at what I have in my yard: a *taraxacum asteracea*. Wow! Isn't that something!" We'd dig up the ground around it, lay down mulch and put a little white fence around it and warn our children not to go near it or else. That's what we'd do if dandelions were fragile and needed us to survive. But, since they don't need us, we do our best to get rid of them.

Today is Christ the King Sunday - it is the last Sunday of the Church year before we start celebrating Advent and the coming of

Christmas. Seems to me that Jesus is the *taraxacum asteracea* King. He is the dandelion Messiah. Our Savior grows wherever he wants. He is impervious to disease, bugs, heat, cold, wind, rain and even human beings. We can ignore him, deny him, forget about him, and he still grows in our lives. We find him in the worst possible places, in the worst situations.

Look at the church in the former Soviet Union. The Church had been under siege by Communism for some 80 years and yet Christ didn't disappear. Just like the dandelion, Christ was still very much alive - he was just under the surface.

There is a true story about a Communist gathering. There were thousands of people. They came – many by force - to hear a speech debunking Christianity as a myth and legend. The speaker said it was time people accepted the reality of science and the truth of Marxism. After he was done, he looked out on the audience and noticed a priest raising his hand. The Communist leader smugly said to the priest, "Do you have something to say?" "Yes," said the priest. The leader said, "Alright, but don't take long." The priest said, "I won't." The black-robed priest made his way up to the podium. He looked at the crowd of thousands and said, "Christ is Risen!" A moment later, the crowd of thousands responded in deafening unison, "He is risen indeed!" The priest turned and walked off the stage.

Christ is the dandelion King. Present in places we would not imagine. He makes his kingdom known even in the most hostile environments.

So, perhaps this is what really irritated the chief priests in the story today? Jesus was operating without their consent. Jesus didn't wait for them to call him king.

What was it Jesus said in the gospel of Matthew? When he was coming into town and everybody was shouting "Hallelujah! Blessed is he who comes in the name of the Lord!"? The priests told him to quiet the crowds? Do you remember what Jesus said? "If these were quiet, the very stones would cry out!" And, today in the gospel of John, the priests complain, "Look, we can do nothing.

The whole world has gone after him!" He was acting like someone who didn't need their permission. He was acting like a dandelion king - sprouting up and taking over - and they didn't appreciate it.

Of course, that's what we find inspiring about Jesus. He comes to us by his own rules, not because we deserve grace or because we are without sin. What faith we have is because Jesus sprouts up in places we'd never expect, at times we'd never predict, but in ways that feed our souls.

I suppose that is what makes the world *go after* him, at least that is what has helped multitudes stay with him over the centuries, is what brings us here this morning. We may not see that kingdom every day. We may not feel that kingdom every day, but when we do, we want to tell someone. Because when God comes into our lives, we just want to talk about it. Sometimes we may even want to shout about it. We Presbyterians might be too reserved to shout, but, chances are, there have been times, we wanted to shout, if not cry for joy.

The minister and author, Brennan Manning, tells the story of leading a retreat for six women in Virginia Beach. He said when the retreat began he met with each woman and asked them what was one thing they wanted to get out of the weekend retreat? One of the women said she had lived a devout life or felt she had. She seemed like a genuinely good person, involved in her church, often helping others. She said she was glad to do these things, but she never really felt that God loved her. More than anything, she wanted to experience God's love, to really hear and know that God loved her. Manning told her he would pray that God would answer that pray for her.

The following morning, she got up early and decided to take a walk on the beach. As she was walking along, she noticed a teenage boy and a woman walking toward her from down the beach. After a bit, the boy passed her on her left, but as the woman approached on her right, she suddenly stopped, made an abrupt turn, walked up to her and hugged her. Then the stranger kissed her on the cheek and whispered, "I love you," and walked on her way. She had never seen this woman before and wasn't quite sure what to make of it.

What would you do?

She wandered the beach for another hour still trying to figure out what had just happened. When she returned to the retreat house, she knocked on Manning's door and when he opened it, she said with a peaceful smile, "Our prayers have been answered."

Jesus appears where he will and to whom he wishes and when he does, we often want to tell someone. That's what happened in the story today - the friends of Lazarus and the followers of Jesus wanted to tell someone, "You see this person before you on this donkey? Where that person goes, God is present!"

And, now, we are the ones to tell the world about him. People experience powerful things in their life and they don't know it is God. They see good and kind, inspiring and beautiful things happen in the world, and they don't understand. They don't understand that these are little parachutes of grace.

It is Jesus, the *taraxacum asteracea* King. He is the one who shows up unexpectedly and sometimes even unwanted, just like a dandelion. We are the ones who can say, "You see that thing that happened over there? Well, that's where God is present."

Maybe our experience of God will be like the shout of a thousand people or maybe it will be like a whisper of love from a stranger, but, wherever Jesus grows his kingdom, we may just want to talk about it.

TO GOD BE THE GLORY FOREVER AND EVER. AMEN.

MOTHER'S DAY

Whispered Love
I John 4: 7-21

Just before Mother's Day, I got an e-mail from a minister friend wanted to know what food reminded me most of my mother. I don't know if I helped him much. I told him burnt biscuits reminded me of my mother.

My mother would burn the biscuits at most every meal. It became a family joke. When we would sit down for dinner, one of the first things we would do is turn over the biscuits and look at the bottoms. She did the same with toast. All she could say was, "You know, charcoal is good for your teeth!" We'd say, "No, mom, we didn't know that."

It wasn't just with biscuits that her cooking came out less than perfect. I can remember one Thanksgiving when my mom was in a hurry to get things done and she didn't start the turkey soon enough. The recipe called for six hours at 300 degrees. In her frantic calculating, she figured that perhaps an hour or so at 500 degrees would expedite the process. We sat down to a turkey that was dark on the outside with a contrasting shade of pink on the inside - not quite raw - but near enough.

We filled up on enough biscuits that would keep us out of the dentist office for years to come. I guess for all you could say about my mom she may have been right about that charcoal thing. I didn't have a cavity until I left home.

What I didn't understand at the time, of course, is it was all about love, really. The burnt biscuits and raw turkey were about *whispered love*. See, my mom became a single mother when she was 40 years old. Her plan had been to stay home all day and raise the four children, cook and clean and mend, be a housewife. When my father died unexpectedly she had to go work in the factory. I know she would have liked to have spent her days differently. She had to give up the dream of being at home and instead had to work sometimes twelve hours days on her feet.

She really wanted to give us the fine home-cooked meals, so she tried to find the time to do that because she loved us. But, that can be tough when you work those kinds of hours and have to tend four children.

But, it was love that motivated her. I hear that now. She was trying really hard to tell us she loved us. She didn't always speak it perfectly and we didn't always hear it clearly, but she wanted to make things OK. After a few failed attempts at cooking big family meals, she made a decision to just take us all out to eat. Once again, it was love that motivated her.

As I thought about it this week, it seems to me that so much of love is whispered love. What I mean by that is we have to **listen carefully** to hear the love. At first, we didn't hear love with our mom's cooking, we heard frazzeledness or just the sound of hard biscuits tapping on our plate. But, when we listened more carefully, we could hear whispered love. That's often the way it is.

I think of a couple lying in bed at night who whisper love to each other or they just touch one another's hand and that says it all. Sometimes it is the quietest or most silent act that speak love. Sometimes even in a failed attempt to do what is right, we hear love. It is the hint of love that matters more than the hugeness of the action.

Rachel Remen, in her book, *My Grandfather's Blessings*, talks about this throughout her book. At one point she writes this:

> We bless the life around us far more than we realize. Many simple, ordinary things that we do can affect those around us in profound ways: the unexpected phone call. The brief touch, the willingness to listen generously, the warm smile or wink of recognition. We can even bless total strangers and be blessed by them. Big messages come in small packages. All it may take to restore someone's trust in life may be returning a lost earring or a dropped glove.

Think about it? Think for a moment. Isn't it true that so many of the simplest words and voiceless actions can speak the loudest message and make the biggest difference? Still, small, sweet whispers of love, like a kiss on the cheek or an encouraging word from a stranger.

Why are these so important?

They are important because they whisper God is near. I think that is part of what I John is telling us. Where there is love, God is near. The writer says we cannot see God, but if we can see love, then, we are seeing God. We cannot see the wind, but we can see leaves moving around in the sky and know it is there. If we want to hear the whispering of God, listen for love. We can't see God because absolute perfection is impossible for us to comprehend. But just because we cannot hear God or see God, doesn't mean God isn't there. Think of dogs who can hear things we cannot hear or bats who can see things we cannot see. So, even though we will never see God directly on this side of heaven, we can see glimpses of God. We get can sense the scent of God, like smelling Cinnabons at the Mall long before we find the booth. We can hear the whispers of God in the quietest and voiceless acts of kindness.

I John is whispering, "You know God loves us. If we want to hear and taste and feel that love, we need to love each other, that's how we will really hear God's love. We can do it." Brothers and sisters, here is the wonderful truth - wherever love is whispered, God is nearby and wherever God is nearby, we are changed. Perhaps the most important thing we can do as Christians is to remind one another of the quiet presence of God.

Tom Long in his book, <u>Testimony</u>, tells a wonderful story of Mary Ann Bird. Mary Ann Bird had been born with several birth defects. She was deaf in one ear, had a cleft palate and a disfigured face, a crooked nose and lopsided feet. As we can imagine, life was hard for Mary Ann. As a child she tried her best to fit in, but it was not easy.

One of the things she had to endure each year was a hearing examination called the whisper test. The teacher would call a student up to the front of the class and then ask the student to put their hand over one ear while the teacher whispered in the other as a way of testing the hearing of the child. The student was then supposed to repeat back what the teacher said. The teacher would whisper things like, "The sky is blue." "Today is Monday." That kind of thing.

Mary Ann didn't want to be singled out any more than she already was. She would cheat so no one would know she was deaf in one ear. When it came time to test her bad ear, she wouldn't completely cover her other ear so she could hear what the teacher was saying.

When, it came time for the dreaded whisper test. Mary Ann said, her teacher, Miss Leonard, "...called me up for my turn, I leaned forward and waited for the words and the words I heard God must have put into her mouth - because they changed my life. Miss Leonard didn't say, "The sky is blue" or "Today is Monday." Instead, she whispered, "I wish you were my little girl." "I wish you were my little girl."

Those words completely changed her life. It was because of those words, that Mary Ann Bell decided to become a teacher. Miss Leonard called forth from Mary Ann her true self with a whisper and Mary Ann discovered she was beautiful and brilliant and now she encourages her students to find their beauty and brilliance as well. - all because of those seven whispered words.

When we hear that story, don't we wish that happened in a church? But even if it didn't, wouldn't we be pleased to know that the teacher was a Christian? And even if she was not a Christian, aren't we glad there are stories like these, because now we may leave here this morning wondering whose ear can we whisper love into?

We may hear the whispers of love in burnt biscuits. We may hear the whispers of love is a teacher who knows what to say. Then **we** may whisper love to the world. And rest assured, whenever we whisper love, we are near to the heart of God, and what we will hear will change us.

TO GOD BE THE GLORY FOREVER AND EVER. AMEN.

GRADUATE RECOGITION SUNDAY

Success
Matthew 19: 23-30; Proverbs 11: 24-28

Although I try not to, every now and then I find myself watching a reality TV show. I don't know why I do this? Just telling you feels like I am confessing something sordid. I feel like the Apostle Paul in Romans: "The very thing I hate is that which I do!" I don't know what Paul was talking about when he wrote those words but I do know my choice to watch these shows leaves me shaking my head at myself.

I don't watch an entire show, mind you. Somehow I have determined if I only watch ten minutes it will do minimum damage. Kind of like the five second rule when we drop food on the floor – if I only watch ten minutes it won't allow time for human foolishness to stick to me – at least that's what I tell myself.

I don't know, maybe I am the only one who wonders about this? Maybe no one else is ever tempted by the Real Housewives of Orange County, Swamp People or Million Dollar Listing? I think the one show which bothered me most was "Preachers of L.A." Have you seen this one? Of course, you all haven't. You all are good, intelligent, moral people. In any case, this show is about mega-church, charisma-soaked, high profile, pastors in Los Angeles. I suppose what makes them high profile is their life-style: Jaguars, Rolls Royce, 5 million dollar homes, perfect hair – it may be the hair which bothers me the most.

Here is the catch for me. I find myself wondering, "Why does this show bother me?" Is it their wealth – and if it is their wealth – am I bothered out of envy? If that is the case, then it is *my* sin and not *theirs*. Or, is their life-style such a large contrast with Jesus? I mean their Savior is the same as my Savior. We both serve the same modest Messiah who had no place to call home, no place to lie his head, even in death he had to borrow a grave. These pastors have more places to lay their head than Kardashians have clothes. But, even if my superior moral judgment is correct, something tells me I have still missed my own point. I mean if my criticism of these pastors is that they live in too nice of homes and drive too fine of cars, then some Third World pastor could easily judge me – or us – with as much harshness. Right? All a question of perspective.

Millard Fuller, the founder of Habitat for Humanity, talked about a time he was making a presentation and he asked what he thought was a rhetorical question. He said, "What size house is too big?" Someone from the crowd said, "Any house that is bigger than mine!" Right? All a question of perspective.

So, if our judgment upon those who are rich is because they are richer than us, then the problem is probably not with them.

So, what is the meaning of all this observation?

I have been thinking about success this week. Today is Graduation Recognition Sunday. We are sending a shout-out to graduates and wishing them all the success life can offer them. But, what does it mean to be successful, what are we wishing for them? Does being successful mean having a reality TV show? Does being successful mean being rich? Does being successful mean *living simply* for that matter? I don't know, but what I do know is that in the Gospel according to Matthew, Jesus says it will be harder for a rich person to get into heaven than it will be for camel to get through the eye of a needle. What does he mean?

I remember hearing about a very small gate in Jerusalem called the "eye of the needle." In order to get through it, a camel has to practically crawl. Some believe that what Jesus meant was that a rich person needs to get on their knees to get into heaven, but, then, don't we all?

We can imagine this was especially confusing for the disciples. Think about it: if the most successful people are going to have a hard time getting into heaven, then what about the rest of us smucks? It would be like going to the senior awards banquet in high school. They tell the kid who has received 27 academic awards that she doesn't have what it takes to get into college. The rest of us B and C students get a worried look on our faces.

We don't think Jesus is saying it is impossible to be rich and get into heaven, but he understands it presents a special set of challenges. You remember how the Chinese symbol for "opportunity" also means "crisis" – ever hear that? Wealth is an opportunity that can be a crisis. Although the percentage of people who curse the day they won the lottery is surprisingly high, most of us would like to the chance to win it nonetheless. Statistically, there is a chance that being wealthy can cause more harm than good, but it can also be a good opportunity to do good that others cannot do.

After former president Jimmy Carter left the White House, he formed the Carter Center. One of his stories is about three multi-million dollar companies who gave the money to eradicate Guinea worms. I have never heard of Guinea worms before reading this. But it is the cause of awful suffering for many in Third World countries. The worm gets into the body through poor drinking water and eventually attacks the body from the inside out. It is a terrible plague for millions.

The DuPont Corporation agreed to develop a special fiber that could be used to filter the drinking water. Precision Fabrics Company volunteered to have their production facility weave the fabric and later the American Cyanamid Company gave a worldwide supply of chemicals that would treat the water and kill the eggs in isolated areas.

In 1988 there were 3.5 million people suffering from Guinea worm. In 1995, seven years later, after the work of these companies and the Carter Center, there were only 130,000 cases and most of these were in the Sudan where health workers are not allowed to go.

Carter says, when he went to the DuPont headquarters to report on the progress to the CEO and 600 of their top managers, scientists and salesmen, he showed them a brief film demonstrating the miraculous results, and by the end of the film, most of them were weeping. All about perspective.

If they didn't have a profit motive to begin with, and if they were not concerned about being financially successful, they couldn't have earned the millions of dollars. If they hadn't earned the millions of dollars, they couldn't have helped those people.

Proverbs 11 says that an amazing thing happens when we give, the more we give, the richer we get and the person who waters, will himself be watered. Likewise, I don't hear Jesus saying we shouldn't be rich, I hear him saying the more we have, the more of a challenge it is to use it responsibly.

We are Christians because in the life of Christ we have discovered a certain kind of abundant life. Jesus says, "I have come that you may have life more abundant." Whatever a more abundant life is, we're sure it has something to do with being happy and our success at happiness in the end comes through caring about the happiness of others.

TO GOD BE THE GLORY FOREVER AND EVER. AMEN.

LABOR DAY

The Blessing of Work
II Thessalonians 3: 6-18

A couple winters ago when we were getting so much snow, there was a Calvin and Hobbes cartoon. Calvin was complaining about being stuck in the house. At first, sitting around watching TV was fine, but then he got cabin fever. His father says, "If you are bored, go outside and shovel snow. It will build character." Calvin grabs the shovel and heads out the door. He says, "How come every time **you** suggest something to *build character* it ends up *feeling like* **work to me**?" Sometimes that's the way it is. Whether or not it builds character, sometimes work just feels like work.

The Christians in Thessalonica had a problem with work. Or, at least, they had a problem with some people who didn't want to work. Ironically, it was their faith that got in the way of their work. They believed what they had been told about the Second Coming. They expected Jesus at any time. I mean any moment. I Thessalonians says: "...the Lord himself will descend from heaven with a cry of command, with archangel's call, and with the sound of the trumpet of God. And the dead in Christ will rise and we who are alive...shall be caught up with them in the clouds to meet the Lord in the air." (I Thess. 4:16-17)

They could already hear the hoof beats of the four horsemen of the apocalypse. They had their bags packed and they were already singing, "When the roll is called up yonder I'll be there." Some people weren't ready for Christ's return. They were.

That was the problem.

As we can imagine, with all these monumental things about to happen, with the immanent return of Jesus, listening for hoof beats and watching the sky, how could anyone expect them to take time to mop the floor in the church kitchen? We can see how it could seem a little, well, **anti-climactic**, can't we? And there was the problem. Why bother doing any of those mundane things when they could feel the first few drops of rain before the storm? With Jesus being so close, why do anything, but just - wait?

So, many of the Christians in Thessalonica, said, "Why bother helping those in need, why bother feeding the hungry, why bother working on church committees, why bother moping the floors, why bother doing much of anything, if Christ is coming at any moment?" Work was just getting in the way of what was important. So, some just didn't work. That was why Paul was writing.

And, I suppose, for us, there are times when work does seem like something we do while waiting for something better, doesn't it? Maybe we are not waiting for Christ's return, but there have been times when we have waited for the clock to strike five so we could go home, or we have been counting the days until retirement. How many times do we see commercials promising this investment or that investment will help us save the money we need so we can quit working? We get the sense that work is the enemy. Work is the four-letter distraction.

Of course, it isn't always this way. Work wasn't always that way for us. It sure wasn't always that way in the Bible. You know it is interesting. When we think of the Garden of Eden, we think of a place where Adam and Eve did nothing but wander around. Before eating of the tree of the knowledge of good evil, we aren't sure what they did? Listen to Genesis 2:15 – this is before they ate from the tree - the writer says, "The Lord God took the man and put him in the garden of Eden **to till it and keep it**." Did you hear that? Even in the ideal world, work was part of God's plan; there was something inherently good about work from the very beginning. Work wasn't worshiped, but work was one way to worship God. So buildings and bridges, churches and cathedrals were built with special care because they were gifts to God.

Work wasn't always our enemy either. Do you remember being little and wanting to work? My grandfather was a handyman – with about any tool you can imagine. A chance to work with him was a great honor. We would fight amongst us over who would get a chance to use grandpa's riding mower. We were like Huckleberry's friends fighting over the whitewash. When adults gave us responsibility, it was like a rite of passage. Remember that?

Years ago I took a group of youth and adults on mission trip to Pittsburgh. We worked at a shelter for women recovering from addictions and their families. Most of the children were younger; they were four, five and six. But there were two African American boys, closer to ten years old at the House. One of our projects was to patch broken cement in their courtyard. When we started to work, we asked these older boys to give us a hand. At first, they were not too sure about this - *they were like Calvin wondering if we were trying to build their character.* As they got involved mixing the concrete and patching the holes, you could see their attitude change. They were enjoying the work. In fact, when it came time for them to leave they complained to their mothers. They wanted to stay and work.

Work is not always a burden. It is our chance to grow up, express ourselves, make the world a better place and perhaps, give something special to God. Work can be a good thing.

The problem with work, for most of us, isn't that work is hard. I think most of us can handle hard work, what makes work cursed and toilsome and thorny is when work seems meaningless. I read an article not long ago that said the number one cause of clergy burnout is not the work-load, but the lack of connections. By that, the article meant, the less ministers feel their work matters to other people, the harder the work becomes. I suspect that's true no matter what we do for a living: when we get the feeling we don't matter to other people or that the work we do doesn't matter, it goes from being a joy to being a curse.

The question becomes – how does our work matter? What makes it holy? Work is holy – it was part of God's plan from the very beginning. No matter what kind of work we do, it can be sacred.

Someone once said that, "To create is holy, because it is the only thing we know about God." God creates. Anybody can destroy, but only God can create and so any time we are creating, we are continuing the work of God. God rested on the Sabbath, but God asked us to give God a hand come Monday morning.

The Apostle Paul was critical of people who didn't work because they were missing their opportunity to create. Didn't matter what they were creating, whether it was a clean house, a decent sermon, a tuned car, or a lesson plan, doesn't matter what we do, it matters that we do it well. The insight comes when we can see how God uses what we do, to bless people. Like the orthodontist who used to say, "I put braces on people's teeth." Then she changed it to, "I help people have smiles and feel good about themselves." That is holy work. Think of a mover who says that he considers his job holy work because he knows how anxious people can be when they go to a new place. He talks to them about all the new opportunities God will provide them. That is holy work. I had a friend who worked for the department of transportation, she spent most of her day attending meetings and establishing grants, but, if you ask her what her job is, she will tell you, she is helping people to get home safely. That is holy work. So many of the jobs we have and the things we do, God uses to bless people. And, if we can stop to think about it, maybe our work will take on a whole new meaning and a whole new purpose.

Sometimes work is just work. But more often, even in the work, there is something holy. Come Monday, God will need our help again.

TO GOD BE THE GLORY FOREVER AND EVER. AMEN.

STEWARDSHIP SUNDAY

What Size Potatoes Are We Planting?
Luke 17: 11-19

Before reading the Scripture, I want us to notice something in Luke:

Today, I would like you to follow along with the Scripture as I am reading it, if you can. I think it will help us notice what is important.

The first thing to notice is Jesus doesn't heal the lepers and then tell them to go to church to show their appreciation. They still have the leprosy when they leave him, but he tells them to go to the priest, go to church, Jesus says. "Go as if everything is going to be OK, go as if you have something to be thankful about," and they go. That, in itself, is kind of amazing. They went. We don't know how long they have been lepers. We can imagine that for some, they would be so desperate to try anything. They'd even try to faith. But, we can also imagine, that if you had been a leper for very long, maybe you gave up on faith a long time ago. But, they all went. If it says anything, perhaps it says a lot about how charismatic Jesus was. He inspired so much faith that all ten were willing to go just because he said to do it.

Now, here is where the story gets interesting - according to Luke in verse 17 all ten were *cleansed*. But in verse 18, only the tenth leper was *healed*. The Greek word for *healed* actually means *made whole or made well*. So, although the other nine had been *made better*, something different happened to the tenth leper. When he saw he was better, he came back to thank God; then, he was *made complete*. What is also telling is the Greek word for *healed* is the same word for *salvation*. The tenth leper was *saved* when he gave thanks. It was gratitude that changed the tenth leper.

All of us have been blessed in one way or another. Even with all the scars we have, we have been blessed. What really changed the tenth leper was saying thank you. He was made better when he listened to Jesus. But he was saved when he said, "Thank you.

Not too surprising this time of year, we saw some combines out in the fields bringing in a harvest of one kind or another. It reminded me of a Peanuts cartoon. We see Violet walking with Charlie Brown and Snoopy is trailing behind. Violet says to Charlie Brown, "Sooner or later, Charlie Brown, there's one thing you are going to have to learn in life: You reap what you sow! You get out of life exactly what you put into it! No more! No less!" In the last frame we see Snoopy thinking and he is saying to himself: "I'd kind of like to see a little more margin for error." I think we'd all like a little more margin for error.

See, we know there is something to what Violet says, "We reap what we sow. We get out of life exactly what we put into it." We don't have to be farmers to know that if we only put in little effort we only get little results. Doesn't matter what we are talking about either: Could be our business, our marriage, our church. We get out of life what we put into it. Little investments often mean little returns.

A while back I read an article on stewardship. The article was titled, "Are You Planting Small Potatoes?" The article begins with a story about potato farmers centuries ago in China. Apparently these farmers didn't use seeds. They would cut up some of last year's potato crop into small pieces and plant them in the soil. The potato pieces would grow and produce more potatoes. They did this year after year until at one point someone got a bright idea of sorting out all of the largest potatoes to eat and keep just smallest potatoes for planting.

We can already predict what was going to happen, can't we? They didn't know anything about genetics, and, as you guessed, after a few years of doing this, they found that ALL the potatoes they grew were small. By eating all the biggest ones and planting only the smallest ones, before too long, all they were reaping were small potatoes.

Not hard to glean the moral of this story, is it? If we invest only small potatoes in our business, our marriage, our church, what do we get back? Small potatoes. Whatever our investment: money, love, faith - life gives back what we put into it. As Violet says, "You reap what you sow! You get out of life exactly what you put into it." There may be something to that.

Now, we know talk about money is a sensitive thing - maybe even more so in worship. Today is Consecration Sunday. It is one of those days we are supposed to think about money. It is interesting, really, Jesus talked about money more than almost any other topic, but we don't like to. None of us like the suggestion we are not giving enough to our church or that we ought to give more. But we especially don't like being told we need to give more if in fact we DO need to give more. It's interesting. What I have noticed over the years is usually the folks <u>who are giving</u> to the church or <u>who want</u> **to give more** are <u>not</u> offended when asked to give more. But, if someone asks us to give more and we find ourselves offended, it may mean it's because we feel we are *not* giving enough.

Several years ago, I served in Kentucky as the associate pastor. The pastor of the church preached a stewardship sermon. At one point in the sermon he told us he tithed. The Bible calls us to give 10% of our earning back to God's work. So, he told us he gave 10%. He told us that because he didn't feel it was right to ask other people to give 10%, if they didn't know he gave 10%.

Now, and this is important, I don't remember him saying that in a bragging kind of way, he just said it to let people know it could be done. But, I remember feeling offended. I'm thinking, *"Who was he to stand up there and talk about giving 10%!."* It wasn't until much later I realized the real reason I was offended. I was offended because I felt guilty. I knew I wasn't giving enough. I was embarrassed. I was ashamed. But, **he** wasn't *making* me feel self-conscious. He just brought to the surface something I already knew in my heart: I needed to deal with my giving and be more intentional, and, I didn't like him stirring me to think about it.

I will never forgot that sermon.

After that moment I made a commitment: <u>every year I was going to give 10% more each year than I gave the year before</u>. It took me about ten years, but after a time, I was tithing, and what is most interesting to me, I didn't feel I was under some great burden. Instead I felt less burdened.

I know people who do give 10% - they tithe. Some of these people are what we might consider rich and others are what we might consider poor. But, I have noticed all of them have a certain peace about them.

We have probably heard it said, if we want to know what is important to someone, look at their checkbook. Where our money is, there is our heart also. There is truth to that isn't there? Where do we spend our money? Where do we plant our potatoes? That will tell us what is important. I know that's true for me and I suspect that is true for you. I want to give more to the church, because I want my heart to be where God is.

I hope you hear what I am saying in the manner I pray I am saying it. Maybe we cannot suddenly quadruple our giving in one year, but we can give at least 10% more than we did the year before and for most of us, that 10% is a very reachable goal. I think we should plan our giving to the church just like we plan to pay the mortgage or we plan for vacation or we plan our car payment.

We don't go to the bank, walk up to the teller to pay our mortgage and say, "Let's see, what do I have in my pocket?" Which is sometimes what we do in church. Instead, we set aside our offering in advance like we do everything else which is essential.

Talk about money in the worship is a sensitive thing. If I have offended you I am sorry. BUT, if your offense was like the offense I had years ago, I pray your offense will move you to a greater commitment.

I pray as we think about our pledge, we will think about how we can say, "Thank you," to God. If we are sowing *gratitude*, we will reap *wholeness*. May God so inspire us all.

TO GOD BE THE GLORY FOREVER AND EVER. AMEN.

BAPTISM

Remember the Image
Mark 1: 9-11

Today we baptized a little boy. In some ways it is like all the other baptisms we have witnessed in our lives. The little one is dressed up. The parents are praying the child doesn't throw a tantrum. The minister is hoping to avoid spit-up on his robe. The congregation is happy to see a family confirming their faith. It is a dramatic event. The best thing which can happen is we see a child smile and laugh. The worse thing which can happen was like when I went to baptize a baby girl and her two-year old brother (whose family had never brought him to church before). He decided he didn't want to participate so he ran around the sanctuary. When asked if he wanted to join us, he yelled, "No, I do not!" So, short of a repeat of that episode, we will have a lovely affair.

In the passage today from the Gospel of John, we read about Jesus' Baptism. I wonder how often Jesus thought back to that moment when he was baptized? I wonder how many times he just stopped and remembered? Maybe when the disciples were arguing or when he heard talk about how people wanted to kill him? I wonder if when everyone around him wanted to tear him down, if he stopped to remember his baptism, and hear the voice of God say, "You are my Son, the Beloved, with you I am well pleased."?

I suppose for most of us, we don't remember our baptism because for most of us were baptized as infants. There is a good reason for that, of course. The reason we Presbyterians baptize infants is because we want to say that even before we are old to start thinking about God, God is already thinking about us. Baptism is not about how we finally have the sense to choose God, Baptism is about how God chooses us when we don't have any sense at all. That seems so clear in the story today. It is not so much about how Jesus made a decision, it is about how God was choosing Jesus even before he knew he was being chosen.

There's nothing wrong with waiting until we are adults to be baptized, but if we are waiting because we think we will be mature enough to finally "get it," truth is, we never truly "get it." At best, we get it for a moment or two, and then we lose it again. And usually, when we do "get it," what we get is the realization, that, "God loves me after all!" We don't realize our brilliance, but realize just how precious we are to God in spite of our foolishness.

My family attended a conservative church that taught if a person died without being baptized, they would go to hell. So, we were told we shouldn't wait. I can remember my grandmother fussing at my older cousins when they began to have babies. The moment mother and child were home from the hospital, my grandmother would start in on them: "You, have to get that child baptized right away! What if something happens?" As you can imagine, that isn't something new mothers want to hear. So, they had their babies baptized right away, if for no other reason, so that they wouldn't have to hear our grandmother.

Now, we don't believe that as Presbyterians. We don't believe that Baptism is necessary for salvation. We believe that Baptism is a sign of salvation. Salvation happens even if we don't have a Baptism.

We think of it more like a birthday party. We turn older each year regardless of whether or not we have the birthday party. The party just makes it more fun. Such is salvation and grace – God provides them without a baptism. Baptism is just meant to celebrate what God is doing and to remind ourselves that in midst of this life – which can be awful and awfully painful - that there is a God who pursues us.

In some ways my family just missed the point. They put too much emphasis on what WE do while the sacrament is about what GOD is doing. The one thing they did get right, I think, is the urgency of baptism. I do think they were somehow right about the urgency, but just for the wrong reason. They felt it is urgent because if we didn't do it, we were destined for hell. It was urgent for another reason. For the same reason all the gospels talk about it right at the beginning of their story, as if to say, this is so important, we just can't wait to tell you. It sure wasn't the first thing that happened in Jesus' life, but it was an essential thing. So, it was the urgency that comes with wanting share something good.

Have you ever had that kind of urgency? We want to do something right now or say something right now because if we do, it will be a joy? It is like the urgency we have to tell someone we love them, so urgent the words almost force themselves out of our mouths. Or like the urgency we feel when we want someone to open a special present we bought them for Christmas. We couldn't wait to say or do something good.

I think that is the urgency of baptism. My family was right about that. Don't wait to be held before the people of God and have the whole world hear what Jesus heard, "You are my beloved child, with you I am well pleased." And you will be my beloved child regardless of what you do, where you go or who you become. It is an urgent message most of us need to hear this morning. "You are my beloved."

Years ago I read a story about how in 1957 a group of monks from a monastery in Thailand had to move a clay Buddha from their temple. The monastery was being relocated to make room for the development of a highway. The Buddha was very large, weighing over 2 and half tons. They needed a crane to move it, but as the crane began to lift that giant idol, cracks started to form on it. On top of that, it was beginning to rain. The monks were worried about the Buddha and so they lowered it back to the ground and covered it with a large tarp to protect it from the water.

Later that evening one of the monks decided to check on the Buddha. He shined his flashlight under the tarp and when he did, he noticed a little gleam shining back. As he took a closer look, he realized there was something underneath the clay. He grabbed a chisel and gently chipped away some of the clay. The more he chipped, the more the gleam grew brighter until after many hours, he stood face to face with a solid-gold Buddha.

Historians believe that several hundred years ago, the Burmese army was about to invade what was then known as Siam. The

Siamese monks realized that they were soon to be attacked and so they covered their precious golden Buddha with an outer covering of clay in order to keep it from being recognized and looted by the Burmese. Evidently, the Burmese found the temple and killed all the monks. So, the well-kept secret of the golden Buddha remained a secret until that night in 1957.

In a sense, we are like that golden Buddha, God made us in God's image and underneath all mud and muck of life, the sins we commit and sins laid upon us, is the holiness of God. We cover ourselves to protect ourselves from hurt. Sometimes the things we did in childhood to protect ourselves don't help us anymore. After a time, those things we did to cover ourselves can harden like clay and the beautiful, golden, Christ-like nature, can be lost to the visible eye. It can even be lost to us. Baptism is a reminder that underneath all that sinful, hurtful, earthy and human covering we wear, is a divine essence. Baptism says that if we wash that all away, what we will find is beautiful. The sooner we peel off that clay, the better we are. The sooner we can celebrate the image beneath the dull, lifelessness that sometimes shrouds us, the happier we will be. God doesn't want us to confess our sins to bring us down, God wants us to confess our sins so we can be unburdened by them. Not confessing sins won't make them go away, denying the existence of the clay, doesn't make it disappear. Claiming it and asking God to remove it, is our salvation.

I pray we see you all here again. I do. But, even more, I pray that somehow all of us hear what Jesus heard: "You are my beloved. With you I am well-pleased!"

TO GOD BE THE GLORY FOREVER AND EVER. AMEN.

ORDINARY TIME

Taking A Risk
Matthew 25: 14-30

I heard of an off-Broadway play that begins with all the actors wearing hats. The good guys are wearing the white hats and the bad guys are wearing black hats. So, we know who everyone is. All is fine until the second act. The actors come out and they have switched hats. So, now we can't tell who is the good guy and who is the bad guy. Well, at least in the parable, we know who the bad guy is, right? The bad guy is the servant who went off and buried the money the master left him. He's the bad guy.... at least we think he is.

It's one thing to try and fail, but to do nothing seems like a waste. The last servant didn't even try. There's a drug abuse commercial which shows two guys in their twenties sitting in cluttered bedroom smoking pot. As they watch TV, a drug abuse commercial comes on TV. The one guy says to the other, "I don't know what's the big deal. I've been doing drugs for years and nothing's ever happened to me" About that time we hear a door shut. Mom's home. She yells up the stairs, "Johnny, did you go looking for a job today?" "No, Mom, I didn't feel good." The commercial ends with a blank screen. A voice says, "If you want nothing to happen to you, do drugs."

If we want nothing to happen in our life, do nothing. Play it safe. So goes the third servant who thought it was much better to play it safe and bury the money.

Of course, the people we respect are those who give it their all. The people who don't hold back, they are the ones we admire: the teacher who gives extra time to help a student; the college student who works for Habitat for Humanity on spring break; the parent who reads to their child every night before going to bed; the friend who is always willing to listen; the minister who is there at a moment's notice; the veteran who went off to war.

The everyday heroes are the people who don't play it safe.

My home church was in a very small town. In order to pay the bills, they shared a minister with another small church. When the minister left those two churches a few years ago, he moved to serve three churches for about the same pay.

Don't we respect those people who tirelessly give and don't count the cost? They are the good and faithful servants, who took a risk and invested the master's money.

Now, I guess there are two reasons why we could end the sermon right here. The first is because we could get home early, which isn't such a bad reason. The second reason is because at first glance, that's all there is to the parable. The parable seems to say - we all have talents: maybe some of us can dance, some of us can sing, some of us can play the tuba, so we should put our talents to good use. If we do, the good will be multiplied and everyone will be happier. If we don't put our talents to good use, then, like the master in the parable, God will be unhappy with us. So, we could stop right there, because most of that is true. God gives us gifts. God want us to use them and we are all happier when we do.

But, there is something else to this parable. It's a set-up, really. We think the third servant is lazy. He should have at least put the money in the bank for interest, right? What we don't realize from reading the parable is that the last servant was actually the <u>most responsible of the three</u>.

You see, according to Rabbinic Law, at the time, whoever buried property entrusted to him, without delay, was not be liable if it was stolen. In other words, the last servant did what was prudent. He was not as irresponsible or as lazy as we might think. The truth is he is very responsible.

Think about it. The first two guys take a big risk with money which wasn't theirs. They seem like those bank executives who were happy taking risks with other peoples' money. The last servant knew better. He knew that the master was a hard boss and there was no way he was going to take that risk. He knows what might happen if the money is lost. So why take a chance? Bury it. The first two servants don't seem the least bit afraid. They take the money and invest it. They take a risk. They act fearlessly.

The third servant is responsible, careful. He knows where to draw the line. As a servant, he does the **right** thing. But, look what happens. For all his carefulness, for following the Law of the time, the master threatens to throw him out into the unemployment line where there is gnashing of teeth.

So, you see, if this parable is telling us anything, it is that the real threat to our faith is *complacency*. The real threat to our soul is *indifference*. Someone once said, "The real spiritual danger lurks not in our weaknesses, but in our strengths." The spiritual danger for most of us is not irresponsibility, but that we are so responsible to the point of being unfaithful. Maybe we are so aware of responsibility that we are afraid to act in faith, so instead we play it safe and do nothing.

Have you ever had something so special or so valuable you couldn't keep track of it? I lost both my high school and college rings, because I kept trying to keep them safe and in the process I lost them both. Instead of wearing them all the time, I only wore them on special occasions, so I eventually lost track of them while trying to keep them safe. Maybe that's a parable about practicing our faith?

Listen, something tells me that when we are facing our final judgment before God, God will not say to us "You took too many risks for the sake of the Gospel." Rather, God will say to us, "Why didn't you take more risks for the sake of the Gospel? Why didn't you go out of your way to be kind? Why didn't you do everything you could to help as many people possible with the resources I gave you? Were you so worried about whether or not I would provide - is that why you squirreled away so much?"

Maybe there is no risk-free choice? If we take no risks in life, we are playing it safe. If we are careless, that may not be much better. But, it is safe to say, there are times God wants us to step out in faith, right? Every now and then, we need to be fearless and we need to spend the treasure God has provided - however we understand that word.

O Lord, let us not bury ourselves in fear… help us take a risk.

TO GOD BE THE GLORY FOREVER AND EVER. AMEN.

Attractive Prayer
Mark 4: 35-41

I've never been much of a fisherman, but my father and grandfather were. My grandfather had a camper he used for fishing trips to Canada. My father traveled a lot for business. If he saw a promising stream he would stop and take out the pole and tackle box that he kept in the trunk. Even though I am not much of a fisherman, there's one thing I learned from them and that is there are certain kinds of bait to attract certain kinds of fish. Worms catch catfish. Lures catch bass. Fly fishing is what we use to catch trout. And, what's more, you can't catch anything from your living room sofa - which is my problem.

I titled the sermon "Attractive Prayer," because I am wondering if maybe certain kinds of prayers attract God's attention? Now, I know this image of prayer as bait is already troublesome. But isn't it true, that when we pray, we feel like we are praying to attract God? "Hey, God, look over here! Can't you see what's happening to me? Don't you care?" Sometimes prayer feels like we are fishing for God. If we read the Psalms, they often sound just like that. Psalm 88:14, says, "God turn your face towards us - look over here!" Psalm 13 begins with the same phrase four times in a row, "How long, O Lord!" "How Long, O Lord!" The way they are repeating they sound like our church bells chiming for attention. So, this idea of prayers as attracting God is not new.

Now, it's easy to see why the disciples wanted to attract God that day on the lake. Jesus had finished a day of preaching. They are out in the boat. It is calm and pleasant. One moment the words of Jesus are soothing them and the next moment everything changes: thunder is booming, lightning is flashing, rain is tearing at the sails. The boat is flooding with water. It's not too hard to imagine the disciples might have felt flooded with fear.

And how confusing! But, "We are right here with Jesus! Bad things are not supposed to happened to us! We try to do the right things.

We aren't bad people. We are church people! How could this be happening to us!"

Not hard to imagine how the disciples might have felt, is it?

When we are worrying, or when we are in trouble, it can feel like we are drowning. Right? Maybe the bills are cresting, maybe our marriage is heading for the rocks, maybe our children are wading into troubled waters, maybe it is just the normal winds of everyday life, but, at times, it can feel like we are being overwhelmed.

What I want us to think about this morning is this: what does this passage say to us about attractive prayer? Notice - the disciples do NOT begin with faith. They are a ship-full of doubt. They aren't confident everything would be OK.... even though Jesus was right there on the boat with them. They were confused and scared and not sure what to do next.

So, what did they do? What led to them having faith?

The only obvious thing they had that day on the sea was fear. They were knee-deep in doubt.

Maybe that is part of the message. If all we have to start with – FEAR, NEEDINESS and DOUBT - that is enough.

The disciples were storm-tossed, scared, wet with sea water, and all they knew for sure is they needed help, but it was enough.

I guess if there is one thing we can say for the disciples, it's – "At least they had enough sense – or maybe it was faith – to call on Jesus." Even if they were unsure of what he could do. They knew whose name to call and when they did, Jesus was there. Maybe he was there all along? But when they called him, then they <u>knew</u> he was there.

Notice – first was the storm, then their desperate attempts to bail out the boat, their cries of fear, finally, they called on Jesus, THEN, the storm was calmed. It wasn't until **afterwards**, **after** the crisis had passed, that they could look back with awe, at how Christ had saved them. <u>Their need for help, helped them find faith.</u>

Sometimes, that NEED is all we have.

The truth is, there are times when all we will have is fear and doubt. And our faith will come down to one thing – knowing WHO to call when the times get tough - and that will be enough. Faith is the **act** of trusting Jesus. Even when we are unsure of what will happen next. We use the word "act," here because sometimes that's all we have. We may not have the heart to go along with it. Like the disciples, when we call upon Jesus, it may be because we are not sure what else to do.

I know a minister who went through a period of depression, and during a visit to him a few months after the depression lifted he said this:

> For the longest time, I believed with my feet and my hands and not with my heart. My feet got me to church. My hands held the hymnal, I mouthed the prayers and I did that - not so much because I believed - but because I wanted to believe. It was only in time I began to believe Jesus was with me in the boat all along.

Faith is knowing who to call and doing it.

So the kind of prayers which attract God is need. If there is need in our prayers, God will have need to hear us. Anytime we come to God with a genuine need in our soul, God is hearing us as surely as anyone who truly loves us, hears us. God doesn't hold the weakness of our faith against us.

Even those who don't believe completely or rightly are blest by God.

I want you to notice something else about this passage today. Notice that at the beginning of the story in verse 36, Mark says, "And other boats went with him." Here is my question, "Do you think those sailors noticed the storm blowing in around them about to swamp their boats?" I bet they did. But, it isn't clear if they know who calmed the storm, is it? They were no doubt praying to their own gods for help. Maybe they didn't think there are any gods or God? But, nevertheless, Christ in his love, saved them all.

Karl Barth, the Protestant theologian, was commenting on this passage and he said something like this: Christ even saves those who have no idea they are being saved. God brings calm and peace into the lives of people who don't even consider that there is a God. God often blesses people with no faith at all - probably in an attempt to give them faith, I suppose.

As people of faith, we know who calmed the storm. We know who silenced the wind. Our calling is to say, "Thanks be to God from whom all blessings flow!"

Too often we are like the man who was late for a meeting and he was trying to find a parking place. He was getting desperate and so he prayed, "God, if you will only get me parking place, I will stop drinking and go to church." Well, miraculously a parking spot opened up right in front of him and the man said, "Never mind, I found one."

God hears our prayers even when they are not said in perfect faith. It may not be attractive to us, but to God, hearing our need for help, for peace, for comfort, seeing our need to heal, to grow, is what attracts God. However, we pray, let us pray trusting God will grace our lives with something good and something good to be found.

TO GOD BE THE GLORY FOREVER AND EVER. AMEN.

Something Happened
Exodus 14: 5-31

You may have heard this story. A rather liberal scholar was invited to speak at the rather conservative Bob Jones University. He was explaining to the students that in the process of translating the Bible from Hebrew to English there are often errors made in the translation. To make his point, he used the story of the crossing of the Red Sea by the Israelites. He said, "In most translations, the Bible says the Hebrews crossed the Red Sea. When in actually, the Hebrew word here is not *'red'* it is *'reed.'* So, in actuality the Hebrews crossed the Reed Sea. The scholar went on to say this was no great miracle, since the Reed Sea had six inches of water." Just at that moment a student stood up and shouted, "Hallelujah! Another miracle!" The scholar stopped and said, "What do you mean?" "Just imagine," said the student, "God drowned all those Egyptian soldiers in just six inches of water!"

We don't know if that exchange actually happened at Bob Jones University. But, we do know that the Hebrew word translated "Red," is "Reed." The Hebrews crossed the Reed Sea that famous day thousands of years ago. The truth is we don't know exactly what happened that day. Maybe the miracle was God holding back the water so the people could go free just like in the movies? Or maybe the miracle was the mud grabbing hold of the chariots until the Egyptians were caught in the tide? All we do know for sure was that *something happened* that day. *Something Happened* and they knew God had saved them.

The Bible is a collection of stories of times when *Something Happened*, and the people felt God was behind it. If we can imagine this: More than anything, the Bible is a witness; the Bible is an epic mural with paintings telling stories of when God reached out to us and we reached out for God.

This biblical mural has moments when we fell short - we got scared, like the Hebrews cursing Moses on the edge of the Red Sea or Peter denying Christ the night before his arrest.

But, more often, the Bible delights in those moments when Something Happened, some moment of grace, when the characters in the mural are changed. The crook, Zaccheus, climbs down out of a tree and repays everyone he ever cheated four times what he owes them. Saul who spent so much time tormenting Christians, becomes Paul the great defender of Christ.

Something happened. Daniel walked out of the lion's den. David took down Goliath. Jacob wrestled with an angel. Abigail intervened and stopped a war. Something happened.

To explain those moments would be impossible, but to deny them would be unthinkable. In the end, it doesn't really matter if it was the Reed Sea or the Red Sea. What matters is something happened and we believe it was God who caused it.

We come here to learn about all those times *Something Happened* in the Bible. But we are also here to see where God is painting something new - in our lives and in the life of this church. Because as surely as God dipped His brush in grace and painted on the canvas of the past, God is coloring our lives today.

Maybe this week something happened to you? Maybe today something will happen to you that could change your life forever? God is still adding to the mural through your life and mine.

I want to tell you a about a few times when something happened and I was there.

At one church I served, a beloved member died. With the money she left the church, we decided to do something in her memory. As a social worker, she often helped women who were trying to escape abusive relationships. So, we donated money to build a shelter in her name. Shortly after it opened, I talked to one of the first residents. For years she had been trapped in a turbulent marriage.

Like the Hebrews trapped in Egypt, she felt like a slave. It had gotten to the point where she felt cornered like the Hebrews backed up against the Red Sea and if she didn't get help soon, her husband would pursue her and it would be all over. And then, she read about this new house. As she sat there in her room, she looked at me and said, "Sitting in this room for the first time was like being in heaven." She could have said, "It was like the waters opened up and allow her to go free." Something happened to that woman.

Another time, I recall talking to a member of my church. She had just returned from working in the Gulf where people are recovering from Hurricane Katrina. She said the first home they went to was so far back in the woods, they had to drive through creek beds to find it. When they pulled up, they found a home teetering on blocks. They looked at each other wondering if was too late for them to turn around and leave?

But, it was too late. The woman who lived in the home came out and said to them, "You are the people they kept telling us would come and now you are here." Then she said, "Seeing you is like seeing angels sent from heaven." Her shy teenage daughter handed them a note which said, "Thank you for giving us the help that up until now we had only heard about."

Well, the whole idea of leaving was forgotten, because **something happened** – not only to the family but to the workers. Does it matter that they didn't literally come down from heaven? Of course not. What matters is that **something happened** that day. God had heard their cries as surely as God had heard the cries of the slaves in Egypt and God had sent people to help them be free.

Last story. Years ago I led a youth group to work on a men's shelter in Louisville, Kentucky. We stepped into this large room a little smaller than our Fellowship Hall – just more narrow – with about 40 bunk beds. They wanted us to mop the floor and clean the walls. We pushed the beds away from the walls and there we saw mold, but not just a little mold, but mold that was black, and thick. I am not quite a germ-a-phob, but close enough. I was repulsed. How could I ask these kids and adults to do this work when I couldn't do it?

Then, something happened.

It was like I heard a voice in my head which said, "Would you clean that wall for Jesus? If this were his bed, would you make sure the place was clean?"

Then I felt entirely different. I went from being repulsed at the idea, to feeling honored. I told the crew to think of it that same way. We are cleaning the place Jesus sleeps. Something happened and we did it joyfully.

I heard a midrash story – a Jewish story about a story talking about Moses and the Red Sea. Andy Jacobs, in his book, *The Year of Living Biblically* talks about a *midrash* version of the crossing of the Red Sea. (A midrash is a story about a story in the Bible.) His Rabbi friend said this:

"We all think of the scene in *The Ten Commandments* movie with Charlton Heston, where Moses lifted up his rod, and the waters rolled back. But the midrash says that's not how it happened. In this story, Moses lifted up his rod, but the sea didn't part. The Egyptians were closing in, and the sea wasn't moving. So a certain Hebrew named, *Nachshon*, walked into the water. He waded up to his ankles, then his knees, then his waist, then his shoulders. And right when the water was about to get up to his nostrils, the sea parted. Then, the Rabbi, said, The point is sometimes miracles occur only when you jump in."[2]

<u>Maybe if something has NOT happened to us recently it could be because we have not waded into the water</u>? We have held back. God is waiting for us to wade into the water.

We are here to learn the stories of when Something Happened. We are here to talk about the times when Something Happened to us. But, what's more, we are here to share the good news of God who makes things happen. We are here to get the courage to wade into the water. If we do that, Something will Happen and it will be good.

TO GOD BE THE GLORY FOREVER AND EVER. AMEN.

---

[2] Jacobs, A.J. *A Year of Living Biblically*, p.13

How Beautiful Are the Feet…?
Romans 10: 11-15

It is basketball season here and almost everywhere I suspect. I grew up in the state of Indiana where basketball is almost a religion. I can remember shoveling snow off drive-ways so we could play in the winter.

John Wooden is one of the most legendary basketball coaches. While at UCLA from 1948 to 1972, he led UCLA to ten NCAA championships.

Most people know about Wooden. But few people know that before coming to UCLA, he was the basketball coach at my alma mater: Indiana State University.

Wooden had a very unique way to approach the beginning of each season. On the first day of practice he would gather all the players to show them the proper way to put on their shoes and socks – that's right – how to wear shoes and socks. He knew that blisters could severely affect a players game, so he made sure they knew the right way to care for their feet. In fact, his wife would wash all the socks at home and use fabric softener just so they were as comfortable as they could be.

We wouldn't think feet would be the topic of his first talk – or even a sermon, for that matter - but, Wooden knew feet were important. Often we only notice how important something is when it is broken. He probably knew the wisdom of the Buddhist monk who said, "When I have a toothache, I discover that not having a toothache is a wonderful thing." So, when playing basketball, it is wonderful to know how to avoid blisters!

But playing basketball is one thing and sharing the gospel is something else, right? I mean we can see why having beautiful feet is important for basketball, but what does it mean when Paul says in Romans? "How beautiful are the feet of those who bring good news!"

We might expect Paul to say, "How beautiful are the **mouths** of those who bring good news." Or, "How beautiful are the **faces** of those who speak the gospel." Or "How beautiful are the **words**" But, Paul says, "How beautiful are the **feet** of those who bring the good news."

Why do you think Paul says that? Seems pretty clear really. If we are going to share the gospel, it's probably going to involve some shoe leather. It's not enough to know the good news. We have to deliver it. It's like the difference between reading music on the page and playing it. Knowing musical theory is impressive but playing a Bach concerto is something else altogether.

"How beautiful are the feet…" It's the difference between thinking about doing something good and actually doing it. It's about delivery. It isn't enough to know the good news; it's the delivery that makes all the difference.

You see, it isn't enough for us to know the good news, we need to deliver it. We need to take the good news of God's salvation to the places where people need to hear it. Just talking about grace and love and acceptance on Sunday mornings is good, but until we can sing it so people can hear it, our faith is just dots on a page. Saint Francis once said, *"Preach the gospel at all times. If necessary, use words."* The poet, Edgar Guest, said it another way: *"I'd rather see a sermon than hear one any day."*

Of course, the Apostle Paul would know that. Paul traveled far and wide sharing the gospel. After Christ first appeared to Paul in the year 37, Paul began sharing the news of Jesus and establishing churches everywhere along the way. He made three long round-trip journeys along the Mediterranean Sea. His fourth trip to Rome, where he was martyred, was over 2,000 miles. The total miles Paul traveled were anywhere from 10,000 to 14,000. Mind you, this is when there were no planes, trains or automobiles.

From that time on, being a missionary meant a person who was willing to put in some miles. The disciples traveled some 100,000 between them. In the 20th century, Albert Schweitzer traveled between and United States and Europe to help the poor in the deepest of Africa. In the 19th Century, it is estimated that the Presbyterian missionary, Sheldon Jackson, traveled all over the country advocating for Native Americans. He eventually settled in Sitka, Alaska, where he almost single-handed saved thousands of Aleut Eskimos. The real irony is when he applied to be a missionary; the Presbyterian Board of Missions turned him down because they didn't think he was strong enough. By the end of his life, when <u>he had traveled over a million miles</u> – they saw things differently.

So, you see, it isn't enough for us to know the gospel. We need to take it to the places where people need to hear it.

The good news for people like us is we don't have to go far to do that. We don't have to look far to find people - people we know right now – who need to know they are forgiven, loved, and accepted. We can go half way across the world to deliver that message - God knows there are places that need it - but we can also share that news by walking halfway down the block or just a little ways across our living room. It isn't enough to know about it, we need to deliver it. The truth is we don't really know WHAT our faith is - until we live it out. The author, and infamous Lutheran radio show talk host, Garrison Keillor once said, **"We can no more become a Christian by just coming to worship on Sunday than we can become a car by sleeping in our garage."**

You see, one of the reasons we talk about our faith is not to convince other people it is true, but to help us define how it is true for us. We put our beliefs into words so they can find a place in our hearts. We put our words into action so they can find a place in our lives.

There is a story that comes from our Christian brothers and sisters in East. According to them, when we finally go to heaven, Jesus will be the first to greet us. He will say to us, "How good it is to finally see you: face-to-face. I know you have labored hard. Let me take care of you." Then, he will invite us to sit down and he will take our feet into his hands and gently and loving wash them.

Now don't we believe it will be good for Jesus to look at our feet and see how they have been used to spread his gospel? We don't want to appear before Jesus with feet that have no dirt on them. We don't want to come before Jesus with church feet. We want to have feet that have been out in the world sharing the good news. We want them to be dirty and scarred and used, so he will know we used them to be messengers of the gospel. We want Jesus to look at our feet and say to us, "How beautiful are the feet which shared the gospel." "How beautiful are **these** feet which shared the gospel."

TO GOD BE THE GLORY FOREVER AND EVER. AMEN.

About the Author

Rev. Dr. Stephen R. Melton is pastor of the Churchville Presbyterian Church in Churchville, Maryland. He has been a pastor for over thirty years, preaching has been a pastor for over thirty years, preaching to congregation of over a thousand to as small as a couple dozen. He learned his style thanks to the teaching of David Buttrick, the Vanderbilt Drucilla Moore Buffington Professor of Homiletics and son of the famous Madison Avenue Church preacher, George Buttrick.

Dr. Melton received the Allen M. Jackson preaching award from Louisville Presbyterian Theological Seminary in 1985 where he received his Master of Divinity. Dr. Melton received his Doctor of Ministry from Pittsburgh Theological Seminary with a paper on developing spiritual discernment groups in congregations. He received a Certificate of Spiritual Formation from Columbia Theological Seminary in Georgia and a Certificate of Supervision from United Seminary in Dayton, Ohio.

Among his joys are grandchildren, carpentry and riding his 1986 Honda Gold Wing motorcycle, including visits to all 48 contiguous states. On the back cover is a picture of Dr. Melton at Deals Gap after riding the "Dragon's Tail" in North Carolina.

www.ingramcontent.com/pod-product-compliance
Lightning Source LLC
Chambersburg PA
CBHW052200110526
44591CB00012B/2021